STORIES FROM THE
GLORY

DESTINY IMAGE BOOKS BY KEVIN L. ZADAI

STORIES FROM THE
GLORY

GLIMPSES OF ETERNITY NOW

KEVIN L. ZADAI
WITH SISTER RUTH CARNEAL

DESTINY IMAGE® PUBLISHERS, INC.

P.O. Box 310, Shippensburg, PA 17257-0310

"Promoting Inspired Lives."

This book and all other Destiny Image and Destiny Image Fiction books are available at Christian bookstores and distributors worldwide.

Cover design by Eileen Rockwell

Interior design by Terry Clifton

For more information on foreign distributors, call 717-532-3040.

Reach us on the Internet: www.destinyimage.com.

TP ISBN: 978-0-7684-5297-6

Ebook ISBN: 978-0-7684-5298-3

LP ISBN: 978-0-7684-5299-0

HC ISBN: 978-0-7684-5300-3

For Worldwide Distribution, Printed in the U.S.A.

1 2 3 4 5 6 7 8 / 25 24 23 22 21

CONTENTS

INTRODUCTION

Thy people also shall be all righteous: they shall inherit the land for ever, the branch of my planting, the work of my hands, that I may be glorified. A little one shall become a thousand, and a small one a strong nation: I the Lord will hasten it in his time.

—Isaiah 60:21-22 KJV

For years, Sister Ruth Carneal has been a beloved friend of mine, my wife Kathi, and this ministry. Sister Ruth is a truly special soul who believed in me long before I was well known. She was among those who served the forty-year, global "gold dust" ministry of Sister Ruth Heflin.

Sister Heflin was a descendant of eighteenth-century revivalist Jonathan Edwards. She has gone on to her eternal rest, but the

1

mantle of glory and worship she had and that her former assistant Sister Ruth Carneal still carries today is preparing to be handed over to the next generations.

Sister Ruth Carneal was called as an apostle, to raise believers up and to carry the Word of the Lord to the uttermost parts of the Earth. She flows in the prophetic and in words of knowledge. Her gifts include a unique, vibrant ability to lead congregations into a prophetic new song.

As in the *Book of Ruth*, the Holy Spirit continues to move extraordinary women (and men) to affect the futures of nations. Sister Ruth Carneal mirrors our biblical Ruth in her dedication and faith and has had the distinct privilege to minister in over seventy-five nations across her lifetime.

People everywhere feel the anointing upon Sister Ruth, even after she visits. Some call her a national treasure. We agree and think of her as a precious Kingdom jewel. It's impossible not to absorb the glory encamped around her as she shares poignant messages of God's love and desire for His children to know and worship Him.

Believers are meant to walk in the Kingdom anointing as holy carriers of divine glory. It is Sister Ruth's passion and life assignment to usher the body of Christ into a higher realm of glory as the bride prepares for her bridegroom's return.

Sister Ruth Carneal and I agree that the glory and presence of God is manifesting in new and greater ways. The Lord is revealing who He is and all He is doing to prepare all people for eternity.

The various stories and prophetic words found within these pages have been excerpted and adapted from our programs and interviews with Sister Ruth Carneal. Many of these are available on *WarriorNotes.TV* and on *YouTube*.

This book is purposely presented in a way that the light of God's glory may shine through Sister Ruth's voice. My views and experiences are largely interwoven with hers. Where necessary for clarity, the text indicates a change in speaker—a slight departure from my usual writing style.

Friends, time is short. The Holy Spirit is quickening our steps to transform minds and move hearts before Jesus returns. We watch in awestruck wonder as our Mighty God weaves an eternal tapestry with our tiny hands and still small voices to reveal His heart and plan for His creation.

Follow the leading of the Holy Spirit as we join spirits, hearts, minds, words, and hands with His. Together we'll walk in the glory realm with a new song of worship and we'll taste and see the banquet of revelation found only while seated in the Spirit around the Master's table.

We invite you to embrace these humble words to usher a greater anointing and revival into your life, so critical for these last days. While we're at it, let's magnify two golden generals of the faith, Sister Ruth Heflin and Sister Ruth Carneal, for their courage and faithfulness to our Father's Kingdom. We honor and extend our heartfelt gratitude to these two anointed "Ruths." May you be richly and eternally rewarded.

With love and affection,

DR. KEVIN AND KATHI ZADAI

One

MOMENTS OF ETERNITY

Lord, we bless You in the name of Jesus. Come and bless Your people in all You have, in every direction. Bless their ears not to tingle, but to hear and know what the God of all salvation is pouring out. Thank You that these are moments of eternity that we are sharing, so that many can step into this moment, day, and hour.

God, that You would crown us with our position and purpose. We decree that all will come to order and begin to flow together. Every member of the family will sit at Your table. God, these are those whom You have chosen to stand amidst the people. Release them to go and do Your calling and bidding. We look to You, the Author and Finisher of our faith, to pick us up and carry us as we go. We declare it all in Jesus' name. Amen.

—SISTER RUTH CARNEAL

THE GLORY REALM

Bless you, saints! It's Kevin here with Sister Ruth Carneal, and we are going to bring you glorious news from the heavens. Sister Ruth and I both feel that the *glory* of God is going to come upon the Earth. It's going to be something that is both individual and corporate. Everyone will walk in this. We have to be carriers of the glory. We can't just have visitations. The days of visitations are coming to an end. We are moving into *habitation*.

There is an atmosphere that God wants you to live, talk, walk, and meditate in. It's an atmosphere of glory that He is moving in. Praise God. Sister Ruth and I are going to help you walk more swiftly toward your destiny by sharing what we have learned, taught, and caught in our spirits.

God said, "Behold, I will do a new thing" (Isaiah 43:19). He wants to bring the atmosphere of Heaven into our realm. God is bringing His people new experiences and new ways to work with Him. A faithful householder brings forth revelations, old and new (Matthew 13:52). Sister Ruth and I pray to fulfill this mandate as we share our thoughts to give you a heart of understanding toward God's will. He wants us to know what He can and will do.

People are asking what time it is. Some say that we are in the last days or hours. We are really in the closing hour of the *moments*. These are precious moments that God wants us to cherish. We are in a period of time when what we do concerns our future in eternity. God wants to reveal how life will be, forever. Right now, the glory of the Lord is being poured out in the Earth.

Let's listen with open hearts and minds as Sister Ruth begins to reveal her story and what the Lord is saying about the glory.

Hello, dear saints. My name is Sister Ruth Carneal. I am privileged to have been raised and mentored by great people of God. A lot has been poured into me over the years. I feel a great responsibility to share what I know.

We can't measure our time on the Earth. It's not even a grain of salt compared to eternity and what God is doing. Do you know that we are on the last seconds of God's time clock? He has our movements on His mind, heart, and clock. We must know that *time is of the essence.* It's time for the body to move with God. We are to use our time wisely. The Rapture will be one-fortieth of a second. We can't even say the word within that time frame!

We are living in a dispensation of the heavens. God is going to reveal His heartbeat to those who are listening. We will want to draw near to Him. He wants us to pursue Him in the spiritual realm, to receive all that our hearts desire.

Our Lord wants us to know Him in a way we have never experienced before. That's exciting! He wants us to have an *intimate* relationship with Him and to love on Him every day. Do you know that He is the best friend we can ever have? He truly is!

Things that happen and that we want to happen typically occur over a lifetime. Perhaps you have waited years for things to happen in your life. You may feel you have missed something, but that's okay. Do you know that even today, God can cause those things to happen in one eternal moment?

I have seen the care that God is bringing from the throne. It can be seen and felt during true worship when God is reflecting in our hearts. God already knows what we are going to do. He wants us to know what He knows so that we can become true worshipers. We are to worship the Lord *out of our love for Him*.

The Spirit of truth must reign in us and be allowed to come out. That process begins with spending time in *intimacy* with the Lord. To have intimacy, we need to take responsibility for our relationship with Him.

Many people don't know how much God wants to be in our thoughts, plans, and daily sacrifices. When we are intimate with God, we won't necessarily see the end of things we are praying for; however, our prayers will cause things to begin. God will even send a word ahead of you because of this intimacy. Intimacy brings favor.

When we don't have an intimate relationship with someone, we must discern all they say and do. We consider whether they are being "real" with us. God is looking for *reality* in us. He wants a real relationship. He doesn't only want people to know *about* Him. We are to know *Him*.

We should be asking questions such as, "What is He like? What does God think about this?" God says that His thoughts are without number. I encourage people to ask Him what He is saying. I question people in my prayer meetings. I'll ask, "What has He said to you today?" We should be asking God what He thinks about our life.

We need to get personal with Him. "Lord, what do You think?" He will answer you. You will feel little explosions or adjustments in your spirit when He pours His glory into you.

Sometimes I hear Him say, "Hmm," just like that. It's very personal. He wants us to be good listeners.

You may wonder why some people fall out under the power of the Holy Spirit while others don't. We have to be energized to a level where we can stand the glory. God is very powerful. His presence energizes. Our flesh can't take the audible voice of the Lord for very long unless we are built up in the Spirit. But when we constantly survey what God is doing and saying, we will have everything we need inside of us.

Scripture says to ascribe greatness unto Him (Deuteronomy 32:3). The praise and worship that comes from our hearts reveal who God is to us. It's how we magnify Him until we see Him. The apostle Paul said that he wanted to know Him in depth and height and width and length (Ephesians 3:18). He is saying, "I want to know You."

One day, the Lord told me, "I want you. Don't linger." We linger in the world. God wants us to linger with *Him*. Linger in the presence of the Lord. Allow Him to search your heart. Let Him prescribe greatness in your spirit, through your prayer life. He is planting seeds in you. Make knowing Him and waiting upon Him your first priority every day.

We are called to be rainmakers. I know you want to be a rainmaker. You want to see Heaven open. You want the harvest to flourish and to see the gathering together of all that God is doing.

We are meant to move into the *ease* of the glory. God wants to show us how to gather, how to participate, and how to *know* the hour we are in. What He is doing in us is for eternity. It's not just for today or tomorrow.

This work began the day you first knew Him. When you first came to the Lord, He began to fine-tune your heart and all He wants (and loves) to do in you. He will show you who you really are and the reason you were created.

As a body, we have only touched a little area of what God is doing. We only live on the Earth for a short while. Our life is a vapor, a degree in the *moments of eternity*, yet look at what God does with those moments.

I once had a vision of the Lord. He was holding a great rock in His hand. It looked like a plain rock He picked up out of the water. I was seeing the end from the beginning. I was looking into eternity. There was a huge smile on His face as He looked at what He held in His hand.

The rock He held is you and me. He has carved us out of the mountain of the Lord. He threw His head back with a great laugh and said, "Come. Let us go up into the mountain of the Lord, to the house of our God" (Isaiah 2:3).

God wants to bring you out of the mountain of your life. This is what you have been waiting for. I saw Him holding that stone. We are called "living stones" (1 Peter 2:5). He was looking at the finished work of what He has handled and what we have tasted, and it is good.

God wants us to see the *movements* of His heart, His love, and His worth in us. He wants us to hear His song, the song of the Lord. There are movements, methods, and instructions in songs. We want to be people who hear. Be sensitive to hearing and seeing His movements.

God knows that He is great. He is the all-powerful Head of the universe. He wants us to call upon Him and to know that His power is available to us. His miracles are available. He heals everything as we allow Him to do it. Give Him your song of what He has done for you. Tell Him how wonderful and great He is.

Today, God is calling us to walk with Him in a greater way. Once in a while, we catch a glimpse of His glory. In the Spirit, I can see a widespread net. There is a great net of the Spirit that God is going to use to pull people into His goodness. It is white, like the Spirit. What God is doing is so holy. Recognize it, honor it, and have great thanksgiving in your heart for His goodness!

Get to know the Lord. Know what He likes and what He has purposed for your life. There is nothing more wonderful and exclusive than hearing the voice of the Lord as you pray. He wants us to learn how to declare Him from our heart as we learn who He is.

Every few months, I give the Lord a report. I write down things I want Him to change in me. Then I get myself ready. I know it won't be hard for God. I write, "What do You think, Lord? Have I passed this test?" Then I meditate on what I have written.

If He doesn't answer, I know that I'm okay, but when He throws a Scripture at me, I go to work. I start washing. I clean up my ways and perfect my words toward others. We want to please the Lord. It's all about pleasing Him. When we please Him, the pleasures come.

The good news is that the Kingdom of God has come! God wants His will to be done. What a wonderful will it is! We can look forward to fully enjoying it one day. For now, we can enjoy His benefits daily if we learn to appreciate Him. Appreciate the Lord in all you do and declare it. Let other people know of His humanity, graciousness, and love.

The bride is being prepared. We are that bride. God is about to bring into our world all that He has created for us. He will see the beauty He has longed to see in us. In the Spirit, I have seen people's chests covered with jewels. God wants to bring the priesthood back into the church. He wants to bring back the true worshipers of God.

The Lord never comes into a church service in the glory just to be there. He comes to bring change, perform miracles, and a fresh anointing. *The glory is the atmosphere of Heaven.* It's the very presence of Jesus doing something in you.

We are going deeper in the Spirit. We are coming into the holy place, the Holy of Holies. His holy presence will forever change you. Things will be left behind that you used to think were so important. We are crossing over into something wonderful!

Jesus said to His disciples, "We are going to the other side" (Matthew 8:18). They didn't really know where they were going or why. They thought about storms and other things. God had to show them. "I will take you through all of this to get you to the place where I want you to be. I'm going to let you endure these things so you can see how I operate." The glory does this. It brings a *knowing*. You will know the Lord and what He is doing.

When you enter into the *glory realm*, at times you act almost silly. Some people don't understand. When a woman is getting ready to be married, it doesn't matter how long she stays up or what time she goes to bed. She is putting on the finishing touches. We are getting ready for Jesus to return.

The very first time I saw the Lord, I saw His face. I could hardly look into His eyes because I was wobbling like a drunken person. I saw the nations in His face. In my spirit, I knew He was revealing my life, my future, who He is, and how He operates.

He told me, "Open the window that is before you." What would happen if we opened two, three, or four windows? We might be raptured! You want to open every window of "self."

The first time I told God that I wanted to hear His voice, I had just spent two hours on my knees. I thought, *Surely He will speak.* He didn't. I heard His voice only when I began to rise from the floor. He said, "I am with you always, even to the ends of the age" (Matthew 28:20). Those were the first words the Lord spoke to me. You will remember these moments that He puts in your spirit.

Open yourself up to God. Don't deny Him. There is a song called "I Would Not Be Denied."[1] I will not be denied. I'm going to have everything He has talked about and more. Today, I understand the Lord more. I'm moving more in His presence. This is very important to do.

God wants to spoil us. He says that all of the other benefits come daily. He didn't say monthly or weekly. He said, "Daily, I will load you with My benefits." That's in *Psalm 103*. It's a heavy thought. I have learned that it's a daily loading. You may feel unworthy.

We can read in the Scriptures about how the wealth of the Earth will come upon the church. That wealth is more than just finances. Those are last on the list. The Lord did miracles and multiplied a little child's lunch! He wants to multiply what is inside of you. When He gives you a word, it's a building block for the great things He wants to do in your life.

As we learn of His ways, we will discover who we truly are—at least in a measure. He said that His ways are past finding out. He tells us, "Greater things shall you do" because Jesus returned to the Father (John 14:12). Hallelujah!

He is multiplying Himself. He said, "Because of the joy set before Him" (Hebrews 12:2). Who was He talking about? That joy is for those He saved. It is for His church. He said, "Delight yourself in Me. I am going to give you the desires of your heart" (Psalm 37:4). Your heart is going to become like His.

God wants to remove all that limits and hinders us. He knows what we need and what is required in this hour. We will be moving with this great cloud of glory, this great cloud of witnesses, and the great army He is raising up.

You will know whether you are walking in the glory or not. Be hungry for it! It will set you free to be as bold as a lion yet harmless as a dove.

THE GLORY WALK BEGINS

Saints, I am thankful to Brother Kevin for the opportunity to share my story about what it is like to walk in the glory. I was raised in Ashland, Virginia on a big missionary training base called Calvary Pentecostal Campground. It began as an eighteen-acre plot of rural land that was given to the family of revivalist and missionary Sister Ruth Heflin. The whole family was a group of pioneers of faith with heavenly orders.

The camp's open-air tabernacle hosted guests from around the world. My parents worked at the ministry. We lived on the grounds, went to school there, and had great training. Schedules dictated our meals, sleep, and prayers. For at least twenty years of my life, when I wasn't out on the mission field, I was up at eight in the morning for prayer. We didn't have church, but we had everything God wanted to do. He gave us wonderful moments of glory.

I realize now that the ministry camp was ahead of its time. The people were so unusual. They had angelic looks upon their faces because they spent so much time in the Word. There was a constant searching out of God, even in me, but as early as age three, I felt different from my siblings and from the neighborhood children.

I was having dreams that I didn't understand. I wasn't mistreated in my family. I was just treated differently. It seemed as if God was preparing me for a life of sacrifice. I didn't think I fit into our family. I wondered if I was part of any family. I would look around just to see who I resembled. I was feeling another world. I didn't recognize it or know how to explain it. Many times, I found myself standing and watching from the sidelines.

My parents thought that I might be ill. They took me to doctors and had people talk to me. It was just God working in my life in unusual ways. He was making deposits in me and getting my attention. That's why I felt different.

Four or five times, the enemy tried to take my life. Terrible accidents just happened. For example, my father was in meetings every Sunday, going from one meeting to another. One day, I accidentally opened the car door while we were traveling. I fell out of the car while it was moving at thirty-five miles an hour!

Most people would pick up their child and take them to the hospital. My father stopped the car, came around, picked me up, and prayed for me. Then he put me into the car, shut the door, and went to the next meeting.

I slept for quite a while. When I awoke, I was perfectly well! We didn't know what happened to me until later when a doctor found some scar tissue. It never bothered me and I never had any problems because of that fall.

We lived by faith. We weren't afraid. My father was a praying man. He prayed over all of his children. We all serve the Lord. Altogether, there were nine of us. My father had his own baseball game, right there. We lived in a household full of faith.

As I said, there was always a kind of searching going on in my heart. When I went to family reunions, I wasn't really comfortable. I didn't interact or join in. The anointing causes a separation. You won't know how to discern it or define it until you get a little older. I now know that I was set apart from the beginning.

I was in church a lot when I was young. I wasn't just going to church. Every church door that was open, I was there. If any conferences were going on anywhere, I was there. I got away from God for a while, but each day I was away, my heart yearned for Him. Every day I was away from the Lord, I knew that I needed to be saved. I wanted to be saved.

When I turned on the radio and heard someone talking about God, it made me cry. If I heard people talk about Him in a conversation, I began to weep. I was hearing from God, but I didn't realize at the time what was moving me.

I was really hungry. God has to put that hunger there, and we have to search it out. You can't delay. You don't get a vision and then let it delay. If you go too long, it will leave you, and if it does, many times it doesn't return. It might be years before it does return—if, in fact, it does.

I also struggled with terrible thoughts about myself. The enemy would put ugly thoughts into my head. *Ruthie, you're nothing. You're dead. You're never going to tap into this thing.* We have to change our words and our way of thinking. Sometimes God uses other people to teach us. That's how my prayer life began.

My mother sponsored many children around the world. I was amazed at how much she gave out of my father's salary to help orphans. My mother loved people everywhere. She used to pray half of the night. I'd hear weeping coming from her room. I would stop up my ears and lock my door when she cried for the nations. She was a forerunner. God wants us to be a forerunner.

When I first started seeking the Lord, I awakened to hear the words, "Prepare to meet thy God." Well, I was young in the Lord. At the time, I thought God was going to take me home. So I said, "Lord, I just got saved!" I lay there for a long time. It seemed like forever. I felt as if I was wearing a straitjacket.

Eternity is in a moment. God can tell you something in a moment that can cover your entire lifetime. I was having some kind of divine shock treatment. I thought, *What does He mean,*

'Prepare to meet thy God'? He was saying, "Learn how to worship Me. Know how to open up to My nudging. Know how to open up to the simple things of the Spirit."

For the first year and a half of being saved, I spent half of my day seeking and searching out the Lord. This is a bit personal, but one day the Lord asked me, "Will you marry Me?" When I heard Him, I thought, *Now, who is talking to me?* I knew it was the voice of the Lord, but I had never heard that sort of thing preached in any sermon, nor had I read it in any book.

When the Lord spoke, I saw two angels sitting to my left. One nudged the other. They both laughed as they said, "She doesn't know who is talking to her!"

It took me a few days to work all of that out. I knew the Lord was asking for a greater dedication and commitment. He wanted to covenant with me. He wanted me to be yoked to Him. You know, when we are baptized in water, it isn't just a theory or a formula. When we are called by His name, we take on the whole of Christ and everything His name represents.

I grew up somewhat dyslexic. I would always write from the back of the book to the front. I struggled to remember things. I could read and study for hours without good recall. I didn't know what was happening. That's just the way things were for me.

One day, God said to me, "Don't struggle with Me. I want to show you My glory. I want to make you a vessel of My glory." When the Spirit speaks, eternal sounds are entering your life. Eternity is revealing what eternity wants.

The Word says that all things are possible to those who trust, believe, and love the Lord. It also says that many are called, but few are chosen (Matthew 22:14).

Few choose to run after God. Few desire to really know Him and love Him. Just trust Him and love Him with all of your heart. The joy of the Lord is your strength (Nehemiah 8:10). You will have daily strength to accomplish all that God is calling you to do for Him.

I had always thought that other people were perhaps a little brighter or smarter than me. Well, God had this to say about it. He said, "I have given you an anointing and a gift of intercession." He said that it is the highest gift and one that is even higher than being the pastor of a church.

Intercessors are the watchmen. There is a lot of responsibility upon their shoulders. Many times, God gives me headlines. I actually received a word about President Kennedy twelve years before he ever took office. I have received words for well-known people, some celebrities, often for intercession. As an intercessor, God puts a great demand upon you to birth things in the Spirit.

My mother and father were intercessors. God would speak to my mother about nations. She didn't really know what to do with what He gave her. I used to hear my father groan when he read the Bible. He groaned and interceded as God parted the waters and made deposits.

The Bible says that unless Zion travails, no sons and daughters will be born (Isaiah 66:8). As intercessors and believers, we are laboring. The stages of labor change to bring forth a child. How we pray, intercede, and even relate to one another, and with the Spirit, changes in the glory. We are slowly being transformed by the ways of the Lord.

That's a "God thing." You can't do that by yourself. One of my mentors, associates, and friends, Sister Ruth Heflin, lived in Jerusalem for many years. At one time, she had thirteen houses there. Even people who are able to afford it don't usually measure out that far or that wide.

I'll just refer to Sister Heflin as "Sister Ruth," although it might seem a little confusing in that we have the same first name. Here is where we differed. In the beginning, I didn't have the faith walk or that "knowing" walk that Sister Ruth had, although we were both born around the same time. My faith grew over time, bolstered by supernatural encounters.

Sister Ruth had many such visitations. One night when Sister Ruth was older, she had a vision from the living creatures of Heaven. The visit took place when her mother was having a visitation with the Lord. She had told Him, "Not tonight, Lord. I'm tired. Would You go and visit Ruth's room?"

The living creatures are the governments and purposes of God. In the Bible, Ezekiel said that he saw the realms in the wheels of God (Ezekiel 1:16-19). Those wheels are the movements of God.

The living creatures went into Ruth's room. That night, a voice in the midst of them told Ruth, "Your ministry is going to change this day. You will no longer go to developing (third-world) countries. You will go to kings and queens and people in high places."

I learned about many of Sister Ruth's travels from other sources. I knew that she traveled, but at the time I wasn't yet active in what God was doing with her. Occasionally I read newspaper articles about her, like when she returned from overseas. Although I had never experienced what she had, I would think, *Oh, I can do that.* I said this even before I ever traveled outside of the city I lived in!

Well, the Lord hears our thoughts. When He says, "I know the hairs on your head," what He is saying has little to do with hair. He is saying that He knows everything you don't know, the things you want to know, and everything in between. He knows the places He wants to lead you into, and the places you will actually go.

When He talks about the sparrow falling to the ground, He knows what is missing and what is needed. God is concerned about everything. He made us. We didn't make ourselves. A great artist, a great performer, or a great developer is proud of his work. The Lord made us to know Him. It's all about knowing Him!

As I matured, I kept searching for God. I didn't run around to different churches. I wasn't running to every move there was. I only went to places where I thought the angel that ministered to me was moving. Over time, I put the dots together and told people what I found. The Lord worked on me for years. He put a hunger in me that had to be searched out. When I finally got saved, He would take me the full measure.

I was once the most introverted person. I took classes just to learn how to speak. I would look in the mirror and practice. Sister Ruth once told me, "I don't know what to do with you." I replied, "Is that good or bad?" The glory wasn't there yet, but it begins to work in you when you step into the action and activity of the Lord.

Sister Heflin lived in Jerusalem but flew in to speak at some of our meetings. She had that glow upon her. Things were easy for her. They just happened. Her presence was that of a giant in the Lord. I can tell you encounters that we have had—Holy Ghost stories. When it happened and when it came, it was supernatural; I wasn't really allowed to talk about it at the time.

Sister Heflin walked in a high place of God. People took care of her. Great people wanted her. Some begged for her to come. She walked in a cloud of witnesses. You want to walk with people who walk with God. You don't have to talk a lot. You don't have to be afraid of what you are going to sound like or that you don't know anything. God will make sure that you learn what you need to learn.

When I began to assist Sister Ruth, things just happened by virtue of helping her. She wasn't hard on my spirit or my anointing. There was an ease being around her. She said few words because she was always listening for the Lord. She walked in the glory. It was as if she was part angel and part human. I know that sounds strange, but she lived in the heavens more than she lived in the earthly realm.

Sometimes I would ask Sister Ruth what she wanted or needed. I didn't really need to ask. When God gave me a date or a little glimpse of something, I would talk to her and she would say, "Yes, that pertains to this or this." I began to align my spirit with hers. We were in agreement, which is so important.

One day, I heard Sister Ruth talk about the glory. At that time, it was just a word to me. Now everyone talks about it. You will know when the glory comes. You become another person—a person of His world. You no longer operate in the earthly realm because the glory isn't there.

You experience the natural, but when you drink of the cup of the Lord there are bitter dregs in there. It's the works of the Lord to know Him, to know the operation of the love of God, and to know the price that He paid. We will partake of His sufferings. Glory is found amidst the sufferings. After all, He is raising us to reign. I had to learn this. At first, I really rebelled. I didn't run. I would just find ways to exit and hide. That's not nice to say out loud.

Listen. You will lose it all if you tell too many people the wrong things. Something probably happened to me in life. To this day, I don't know what it was. At least I knew early on that the Lord really loves me.

I was happy with that knowledge, but I remember how I was. Sister Ruth used to sit on me, like a pillow. I didn't understand why. It was as if she held the reins of my life. I never wanted, nor was I ever trying to take her place. In fact, I waited on her. The glory demands a lot of you so that you won't lose it. Sister Heflin didn't put many sanctions upon my life. Let's just say that people who walk in the glory don't sleep very much.

I helped care for Sister Ruth's needs when she ministered. Sometimes she gave me lists of things she wanted. The lists never came with any money. She would just say, "This is what I need."

We weren't to ask for anything in the camp. Everything we needed was to come to us in a supernatural way.

Sister Ruth once requested a horse saddle! I read the note she gave to me and said quietly, "Yes Ma'am." When I left the room, I wanted to tear up the note. I was thinking, *What is she asking for?*

I remember being upset and walking into the cafeteria. A guest who was seated there asked me, "What's wrong, Sister Ruth?" I replied, "There are some strange things I need to get and I don't know where to find them. I don't even know where to look for them. I don't have any money. I don't know how to take care of this."

The man asked me, "Well, what are you looking for?" I replied, "I need a saddle for a horse." Do you know what he said to me? "Oh, I have one. What kind are you looking for?" Remember, the Lord tells us that whatever we need will be at hand. He will cause angels to appear and send people to your aid. I would watch how Sister Ruth flowed in the Spirit and how she handled responsibility. She never accepted a "no," even when something seemed impossible.

When Sister Ruth first began to speak at our church, we didn't understand the glory realm. But I loved to watch how she always got "meat" out of the messages she preached. Out of those messages came new songs and visions from the Lord and a river of revelation you never heard before.

God will train you with revelation to change the world. He will always use what you learn in some part of the world. He doesn't let anything lie dormant or go to waste that you have gone after. He is a great provider.

We didn't talk about some things with others, because people can have knowledge without power. That isn't any good. There is a dependence upon God that comes with drawing close to Him. You really want to live in that realm.

People who have money can live in the natural realm where it provides for things, but it becomes a weight. That's the weight of the Earth upon you, not the weight of the glory. You want the glory.

When I looked into Sister Ruth's eyes, it was like looking into a pool of water. I felt like I was looking into eternity. I never said "no" to her. I didn't try to reason when she asked me something. I never made excuses. We lived in a place of great faith and change.

The Lord told Sister Ruth that once she moved to Jerusalem, the glory would come. The glory is God's Jerusalem experience. It's a place where angels are charged and God is moving. It's a place where the Holy Ghost is in charge and where there is fruitfulness in everything.

When she ministered, it was as if the Spirit would lift her up on a throne. I have seen a huge angel stand behind her. He wore a sapphire blue suit and had hair like gold. He would move his hands and head when Sister Ruth moved hers.

When she spoke, a triumphant, trumpet-like sound could be heard in her voice. It sounded like many waters. One time in the Spirit, I saw what looked like Niagara Falls pouring out of her. If you have ever been to the Falls, you know they are loud. You can't hear very well because the sound is deafening. You have to yell above the noise just to be heard.

Brother Kevin has said that he has heard a trumpet sound in recordings of Sister Ruth. It sounds to him as if there are voices behind her voice. Her voice was loud and powerful. It vibrated. I saw that vibration and also where it would multiply in all who heard her speak.

People tried several times to correct Sister Ruth. They would say, "Ruth, you've got to change the sound of your voice!" They didn't recognize what God was doing in her. He was using her voice to lift the people from where they were into a new place. It was a holy thing.

God wants to be visible. He wants to be seen. He manifests in different ways through our love for Him. Sometimes I could almost see steam coming off of Sister Ruth. Now we reproduce that cloud using technology. God knows how to manifest it and we need to let Him work.

Even as a young girl, Sister Ruth would hear a word from the Lord and drop everything to obey. She told me that she prayed from age three to five and every day after school, Monday through Friday. She prayed all of her young life. Because of that, Sister Ruth was able to hear the sounds of God and feel His movements in those sounds. She had the ability to feel the currents, flow, and direction of God.

His glory is like the colors of the rainbow. The colors change from purple to green and from yellow to red. They keep changing from glory to glory. You can see a reflection of His character and nature in the glory of the rainbow.

God reveals His glory to us. We see it in greater detail when we praise and exalt Him (Psalm 108:5). Let's declare what He is doing so that others will be brought into the knowledge of God. They will see what they haven't seen before. People will be carried away by the currents.

I learned, exercised, and proved God again and again as I served Sister Ruth. I found that God isn't always predictable, except with His Word and His truth. He establishes truth, but His ways are His personality. He said, "Learn of My ways. Learn of Me and from Me."

There are things only God can teach you. He wants to teach you! When the glory gets into you, it will awaken everything inside of you. You won't quiet that person down. You will come alive and begin to move because of the Lord's holy presence. The glory moves you into action.

I left home to be a missionary. A lot of people thought that missionary life was difficult. I never felt that way. I thought, *Oh, this is wonderful. I'm going to be a good missionary.* Everyone else looked at the natural, the simple. Well, it is simple.

One day, Sister Heflin asked me, "Would you like to travel with me?" I thought, *I could do that.* I was always saying, "I could do that." I never realized that she would just ask me to do things without preparing me ahead of time. She didn't always tell me things before they happened, but that wasn't necessarily a bad thing.

She would wait until the right moment in a service. I could tell by her eyes and her look. She was waiting for a certain moment, like an eagle ready to leap off of its perch. Her words would grab hold of your spirit. She had a wonderful way of releasing the glory at the right moment. Governments were in her mouth and they thundered!

As Sister Heflin and I traveled, the glory was constantly breaking forth in different directions. She wasn't in a whirlwind. She was in the winds of the Lord. She told me, "You have moved into a realm." The glory realm is all about worshiping the Lord. It's not about us.

In the glory realm, you may ask, "Who am I?" You will wonder if anyone knows or understands you. People may think you are strange because you are different. Don't worry. You get used to it. A great ease comes with the glory. It brings forth the ease of Heaven. Things are easy. It seems as if angels escort you wherever you go.

Sister Ruth had the authority of Heaven upon her. Wherever she went, people obeyed her, even though she didn't make great demands.

Understand that God has different patterns and standards for different people. He told Sister Ruth not to study for a sermon. Then He told her, "I'm going to show you My glory. Take your concordance and your Bible into the pulpit, wherever you go. Meanwhile, worship Me all of the time."

Sister Ruth got a new Bible every year so she wouldn't depend upon her notes and markings from the year before. And she would listen to prophecy for the direction it contained. She truly followed the winds of the Spirit. Everything God wants for His people is found in the winds. God will have His way in the whirlwind. He knows which way He wants you to move. When you move in the glory, there are a lot of whirlwinds.

You will wonder what is happening. It's God. Just let it be. Nothing is done unless the Lord lets the wind blow in your life. Allow Him to work. You will be so thankful to be a person from His world, not someone lost in their own thoughts and ways.

Sister Ruth put certain restrictions on my life to help me flow. They did help me, even as I helped her. It's nice to have a ministry of helps. The people with this gifting are the backbone of the church. They are dependable, ready, willing, and able. With them, helping and preparing are never a problem or a bother.

For twenty years, Sister Ruth and I would enter the church sanctuary to pray and praise for at least twenty minutes before a service. We did this to prepare our hearts for what God wanted to serve. We never practiced our songs. We sang new songs that would become songs for the very next meeting. Can you imagine? The Lord was beginning to give us patterns from Heaven. Each service was different. We had pretty good rhythm too. That's because God moves in the rhythms. He moves in the flow.

We always wanted something new, but we didn't know how that newness would come. People do this today but then they question whether the new things that come are really from God. People who know their God will know when He is moving. They will have exploits in their life.

Today's church needs to come alive. It needs to be revived. We need revival. Look for windows, openings in the Spirit, while you sing. Look for the right timing for the glory to come in. This is what the Heflins taught us. The whole family was like a dynasty in the Spirit.

We are to gather from the winds, from the testimonies of the people, and from the words that are spoken. I learned to preach by always being ready. I knew I could be called on by Sister Ruth to preach at any moment. Isn't that wonderful? You just sit and wait. It might be this time or that time. As I waited, I learned to study and to be patient.

One day, the Lord said to me, "I showed you one glimpse of My heart. Because you waited and followed Me, now I will reveal My glory to you. You didn't chase after man. You didn't run hither and to. Because of that, I will reveal My glory to you. You will see how it operates."

The glory is an entirely different atmosphere. We are being asked to move into it. It's a place of God's pleasure. It's where He does what He wants to do. It's the most wonderful experience. Because you will have a meal that God brings, you won't be happy in any other form or fashion. You will have tasted something real and eternal.

God told me, "I shall lead you by My Spirit. Be awake. Be alert. Pay attention. I will speak My secrets and what I am doing into your heart. I want to share this with you." That's something that we all should desire to tap into.

In the glory realm, you must be ready to go at a moment's notice. We don't want it in our flesh. The glory is a little difficult at first. But in the glory, we can know our future, if we really want to hear from God. We can almost know what is going to happen next.

Nowhere in the Bible does it say that when Jesus called His disciples any of them said, "I have to go home and take care of my wife, my cow, or my land." He just said, "Come. Follow Me." If they replied at all in this way, it isn't found in the Word of God.

The Lord is calling *all* people, from all parts of the world, to see what He is doing. He said, "All trees shall see it together" (Isaiah 41:19-20). The trees He talks about don't all grow in the same place. He told them *all*. He is calling all of us to step into His glory and to have our own glory walk with Him.

FINDING MY SONG

Saints, please allow me to continue the story of my walk in the glory. While I was still young in the Lord, a hunger entered my spirit to know Him. I went searching for Him. He eluded me for five years, but He gave me little glimpses of the glory. It was a bit like looking into a kaleidoscope. Do you know how when you turn the dial, things change? You catch a glimpse of its beauty. There are movements. The way kaleidoscopes are made is strange, yet they create beautiful movements and images.

Every time God changes our ministry or puts us in a new place, we come closer to our destiny. What God has for us is breathtakingly beautiful. He wants us to be willing to trust Him so that we can see His plan for our life.

I learned to hear from Heaven through songs. Over forty years ago, the Lord spoke to me in songs about my life. He told me that I was going to be different. He said that He would sing songs over me—songs of light and direction. He told me that I would be going to the nations.

He also said that I wouldn't get what my other family members got. He warned, "You won't be favored in your family." I didn't think that was so bad. I mean, it could have been worse. You have to get the joy of what God is doing. Rejoice!

God uses our senses to declare His glory. It's all about celebrating Him. He will give us a new celebration and a new song in our spirit. Songs would come to me. The melodies and words were kind of downloaded directly from Heaven into my spirit. At first, I didn't understand that the songs were mainly designed to bring the Jewish people out of many nations to return them to their homeland.

God had told me, "I'm going to sing songs over you. I'm going to give you the personality of people through the songs I sing." I thought, "Oh, this is wonderful!" But I always wanted God to say, "Thus sayeth the Lord," you know? I wanted some lofty trumpet sound. That's because John said that he heard a voice like a trumpet behind him.

It didn't happen that way with me. Still, I wanted to be sure of God's voice, so I told Him, "Now Lord, make sure I know." I used to challenge Him. "Now Lord, You've got to make sure that I know. You know that I don't hear very well."

The songs God gives you in your spirit will reveal what He is speaking to you. Through the songs He sang, He introduced me to the idea that I would be traveling. The songs would carry details about a specific country. When I heard them, I knew that God was asking me to travel there.

The Holy Spirit bypasses the natural mind with a revelation of what God is doing. He loves it when we move into these realms. He wants us to rejoice in the ways that He chooses to manifest His glory.

The first songs I received caused me to talk to God about them. They were strange. I thought, *This can't be God. God, You don't really speak like this.* That's because others had taught me "how" God speaks. They would say, "*This* is the way God does it." I had walked in that for a season, but I hadn't seen any miracles.

In the early days, traveling to Israel was never a thought in my mind. I had no contacts there. I wasn't yet conscious of the reality of Israel. The country is truly the time clock of the world. If anything is going on in the world, it begins and ends with Israel.

One day, I found myself saying, "I want to go to Israel." Then I thought, *Now, why did I say that?* Not long after I said that, I turned my heart back to God. I hadn't been thinking about Israel. I just found myself singing a song. I didn't know the words but I began to jump up and down and do some "Lies." I sang, "Lie, lie, lie, lie, lie, lie, lie..."[2]

In my spirit, I knew that it was the key of David. People are trying to find out what the key of David is. *The key of David is the glory.* The Lord told me, "I'm going to return the key of David to the church." He is preparing to do this from Heaven. We are going to dance and rejoice.

David instituted round-the-clock tabernacle worship in the city of David. Think about it. David is the only person in the Bible who (in a way) fed more people than Jesus. Jesus fed groups of four to five thousand. David fed the whole city of Jerusalem with his dance.

David was always singing a new song because he was always fighting a battle. His song was about the end from the beginning. He was getting the victory while he sang. The Bible says, "With a loaf of bread, a piece of meat and a flagon of wine" (1 Chronicles 16:3). We don't really know what that wine was, but David fed the whole nation.

When David entered Jerusalem, the Ark of the Covenant came with him. That is the atmosphere we want to bring with us when we enter a room or even a city. The atmosphere changes when the glory is upon you. You realize it when you speak. It oozes out of you. It pours out and takes you and everyone else into the next realm.

Now that I had this new "Lie-Lie" song pouring out of me, I went to a friend to see if she could interpret what I was singing. My friend was Jewish. She said, "Oh, that's an Israeli song." I just knew in that moment that I would be going to Israel. It was that simple.

As I said, the Lord speaks to me through songs. Once I understood that I was truly hearing from God, He said, "I will sing over you with songs of deliverance, songs of delight, and songs of victory" (Psalm 32:7).

Do you know that every person has a song? We may think that we are just singing and having a merry heart, but that's not all that is happening. The Lord is fine-tuning and preparing you. He is turning your heart toward the heavens and bringing in the heavens.

He says, "On Earth as it is in Heaven" (Matthew 6:10). Many of us have said this Scripture verse without understanding how it applies to us. We are literally going to see Heaven on Earth. It will be coming by way of the glory realm. There will be many adjustments in us in order for this to occur. You see, when we are going through a great trial or rejection, we aren't having mental problems. It is because we have *heart* problems. Our heart needs to be adjusted to God's thoughts.

I have to say that in just three months' time, God adjusted my heart and sent me to Israel. Those three months were the tuning time, the time of my preparation. Israel is a place of surgery. It does a lot in your heart, your life, and your thinking. It's a place of great revelation. It's a place of the supernatural.

When you put your feet there, you are doing more than just walking and seeing where God released His Son to the salvation of the whole world. You will get a river of revelation of how God is moving. You will begin to understand the wonders and the delight that He has in you.

Israel is the tuning fork and pruning place of the Spirit. It's where you hear from God. While I was in Israel, God told me, "I want you to listen to every song that I sing over you because My plans are going to be in the songs." God uses the talents that are in us. I came from a family of singers.

At some point, God sang another song over me. I didn't know the tune at first, but it's a Russian ballet song called *The Swan*. I simply began to hum it. I called another friend and shared the song with her. She knew what it was. She said, "Oh, that's from Russia." Once again, I knew that I would be traveling—this time to Russia. And once again, within three months, I found myself facing a new nation.

God gave me a vision to move to Russia. I find that interesting now, because in the fourth grade we studied geography and history. As the teacher pulled down the maps, I talked to God, not consciously realizing that He might actually be listening and taking notes.

I remember that I had said, "Lord, you can send me any place in the world, but I don't think I want to go to Russia." Well, which people do you think He placed in my heart? I'll give you one guess.

NOTES

1. Charles P. Jones, "I Would Not Be Denied," 1900, public domain. The lyrics are based on Genesis 32:26.

2. "Hava Nagila" is an Israeli folk song. It means, "Let us rejoice."

Two

Opening the Glory

Lord, we bless You in the name of Jesus. Lord, You know what we want and need, but we have to understand. I thank You that as Your Word says the knowledge of God will never stop. What has been hidden shall be revealed in our everyday movements, in the places we go, and as we bend our knees unto You.

Thank You, Lord, for the listening ear. You said You would open the windows of Heaven. Let our hearts be open and receptive to Your whispers. Let there be such a knowing, like a husband and wife, that we know the heart of our husband, Lord, as You want to know the heart of Your bride. Amen.

—Sister Ruth Carneal

ACCESS POINTS

Friends, it's Kevin here. Did you know that you can access the atmosphere of Heaven in your spiritual life, your conversations, and your worship? Yes, you can! Many people want to know how to begin to walk in the Spirit. They are hungry for encounters with God. They want to know how to have access to the glory. Do you know that it is really very easy? We have just seen that you can begin by giving your heart and life to the Lord. When you do that, He will not only cleanse you of all of your sins. He will also begin to speak to you and take you on a journey unlike anything you could ever imagine.

What we need to know is that one of the keys to the glory realm is that there are *access points*. These are things that allow us to easily move into the glory. For example, every church or ministry service is meant to be a divine doorway, a point of access to the heavenly Kingdom.

However, we can't just enter into physical meetings or other places in any kind of way and expect the glory to come just because we want it to. God dictates how we may enter into His glory and into His Kingdom.

To that end, God is trying to reveal things to us in a clearer way. Something better has come. It's not an anointing. We do want God to anoint us. It's the *better* grace. It's the better meal. It's the glory of Heaven.

The glory is the presence of Jesus Christ. The glory gives us access to Jesus. We are seated where He is. In the glory, Jesus speaks with us face to face. We can stand (or kneel) in His presence in the glory.

When we are born-again Christians, we walk in two realms on this Earth. We have a body and a spirit. We are really a spiritual person in a natural body. God is a Spirit. Those who worship Him must worship Him in Spirit and in truth. God has always been dealing with both parts of us. However, a new move of God began a couple of years ago.

Most people have yet to step into the glory because they think there is a prescribed way to enter. In a sense, there is, but entry into the glory doesn't come by way of doctrines. There are divine doorways and heavenly protocols.

Let's listen closely now as Sister Ruth continues to bring forth her insights as to how we may access and walk in the glory realm.

(Sister Ruth's story continues.) I have been called to prepare people to enter into the glory that is coming upon their life. Every day, you want to have something new and different. The glory is a walk that constantly changes. We will be changing throughout our life.

The Lord told me that I haven't yet arrived. I often talk to Him the way a wife talks to her husband. On my way to my prayer meeting one day, the Lord said, "Hmm. Business as usual, hey?" He said it just like that, "Hmm."

Sometimes when you won't receive what the Lord wants you to hear, He will speak to your friend in a dream to get a word to you. Do you know what I mean? He speaks to us in many ways to help us understand His will.

When the Lord said "business as usual" to me, I was driving down an exit ramp. I said, "It won't be that way this morning, Lord." When I got to my prayer meeting, I told the people there, "Everybody on your feet. We're going somewhere with God. We're going to hear from God." In the glory, it won't be "business as usual" because we are entering a time of change.

I shouldn't say that it is my prayer meeting, because it's really the Lord's. He told me to hold a prayer meeting near where I live. I have held it weekly for sixteen years. At the meetings, we pray until Heaven comes down and people see visions. They have an audience with the Lord. You only need an audience of one.

When you know the Lord, you won't be hurt. You won't be embarrassed or ever feel left out. You won't be concerned about what other people say. In fact, you won't even want to know about it. You won't even ask. That's because you will only want to hear what God has to say. We should ask, "What is God saying?"

He is hastening to perform His Word today as eternity invades our time. This means we will do more in a day than we have done in a year. We will do more in a month than we have done in five years. God is moving quickly. In these times, we are going to cut to the chase, shortcuts and all. Shortcuts will be necessary. That doesn't mean we ignore the law of the Lord or even good teachers. But we will learn to do things in greater ways and with ease.

God said that in the last days He would cut things short because of the timing and the coming of the Lord. We will do less than we did before because some things we do aren't in the eternal plan of God. We will be focusing on all that God wants to do.

The Lord favors those who draw close to Him. The closer you come, the more quickly your prayers are answered. The working of miracles takes place in your life. He will prove you when you think nothing is working. There will be quick, exciting "suddenlies" in your life with God when you have been proven, pruned, and prepared.

When you come face to face with yourself and who God really is, you become a worshiper forever. He was, is, and is to come in everything. We have a jealous God. He is jealous over those who belong to Him.

In the days to come, there will be such an increase and move of the Spirit in the world. Whole cities and nations will be saved because we have spent that precious time with the Lord. Our prayer life will accelerate to the things that God wants to do.

We need to learn to recognize the *access points* that help us to move into the glory realm. They are the means by which we enter the presence of the Lord and access the riches of the Kingdom that He so longs for us to receive.

Drawing Near

Saints, just as Brother Kevin teaches, the conversations you will have with the Lord will draw you closer to Him. The more time you spend with Him, the closer you will become and the more you will desire to have intimacy with Him. You may ask how you are to find this intimacy. The key is the glory.

The glory is the key access point to Heaven. There is power in the glory. God works with what is familiar to Him. We are to enter into His presence and dwell there in that secret place with

Him. It's an intimate place, an intimate walk with Jesus that you will want to remain in forever.

Understand that the Lord is everywhere. He is beyond all we know, think, or even hear in the news. He knows everything and wants us to know it too. We are meant to look unto Him.

He said, "I have opened a door that no man can shut" (Revelation 3:8). The Lord showed me the glory at work, when pastors gave me a prayer room at no charge. One said, "Sister Ruth, God told me to give you this room for two years, without charge. The price has already been paid."

The glory doesn't just change your spirit. It changes you in the natural as well. The Lord told me, "I want you to tap into the glory." There is a tapping in that needs to take place. We have to learn how to tap in, to enter in. When you tap into the glory, the currents of Heaven will come and change you. You will find that you will change your mind about a lot of things.

Brother Kevin has taught us that God's ways are often very foolish. The natural world doesn't understand them, but you do when you have the Holy Spirit. Some of God's best servants have no problem allowing the Lord to use their personalities in a way that may sometimes make them look a little foolish. God purposely confounds the wise with the foolish things of the world (1 Corinthians 1:27).

One day, I saw Brother Jesse Duplantis on television. He was wearing a highly polished jacket. I saw the wings on it. Don't you know that I talked to the Lord about that jacket? I will say to be careful what you discuss with the Lord. That's because what is said in the prayer closet will be shouted from the housetops!

I had said to the Lord, "Lord, I think Brother Jesse needs to pass that jacket on to someone else." I don't know why I said that. I continued, "I think he has outgrown it. What do You think, Lord? Don't You think he should give his jacket away?" I'm being serious here. I actually said that.

Sometimes when we think we have outgrown something, God still has plenty of room in there for us to grow. We need to consider the deeper things. And don't you know that God will take your words and reveal His glory through what you have discussed with Him?

There are things we don't understand, waters we can't walk through, and fire we don't want to stand in. Those are baptisms of what God is doing in the Earth. They bring His holiness and commitment into our life so we can become a part of who He is.

We are His bride and His servants. A bride doesn't really want to be a servant. She's the bride. It's her day. Being a servant is part of the ordination of who you are in God. Every servant is a precious facet of God that is working through them. Some people are still stones that are a bit rough. Others are polished gems.

Brother Kevin Zadai and I are good friends. I understood him the first time I saw him. The man has fire all over him. I can see the glory of the gold coming out of him. I can see Jesus shining in him. I see a holy treasure.

You have to see the treasure of what God is doing in people and you have to respect them for who they are. God is working through them. It took me a long time to learn how to respect other people. It's not that I didn't want to respect them. It's just a part of who we are in the flesh.

One day, Brother Kevin came to Arizona. He was wearing this jacket. I thought, *Now, where have I seen that jacket before?* He took it off and said to me, Here Sister Ruth. Do you want to wear this? It belongs to Brother Jesse Duplantis." God remembered what I had said about that jacket! I couldn't believe it. It was the first time God ever arrested me for talking about someone.

I asked, "This is his jacket, the one I talked to God about?" God not only allowed Brother Kevin to wear it. I also got to wear that jacket. Brother Kevin took that jacket and anointed other people wherever he went. Wherever he spoke in Phoenix, Arizona, he put that jacket on others. God's anointing is on Brother Jesse. He has a special, unusual anointing. The anointing is also on Brother Jesse's jacket.

The first time I heard Brother Jesse speak, I thought, *This is a comedian. This isn't a preacher.* But you see, my mind wasn't yet sanctified. My Spirit wasn't yet changed. We can do *all* things through Christ. All of God's servants are unique. He wants every one of us to be a shining report.

When I first saw Brother Jesse, I thought, *Are there clowns in Heaven?* I mean, the man has too much joy to be a preacher! That's what I thought. I wasn't belittling him. I just didn't understand that Brother Jesse had found the key.

Brother Jesse Duplantis has that special anointing. It's something that is everlasting. It rubs off on people. It affects people in a contagious, positive way. That's what you want. You want to affect the atmosphere in a room. You want to let the enemy know who you are.

The glory will carry you into that next place with God. It will allow you to draw near to the Lord. It will carry you into eternity. Brother Jesse tapped into the glory realm. He moves in it. He drew near to the Lord. He has the joy of the Lord in abundance. It's contagious.

We can all use more of that joyful anointing! That's why Brother Jesse has such wonderful strength to do the work of the Lord. Brother Jesse and Brother Kevin both are shining examples of God's bountiful blessings that can be found in the glory realm when we draw near to the Lord.

God wants us to find the currents and rhythms of Heaven so that we can move with Him. To help us, He will shift things and move some things and some people around.

He says, "If My people, which are called by My name, will humble themselves and seek My face and repent, then will I hear from Heaven" (2 Chronicles 7:14). There is more to it than that. We need to hear from Heaven. We need to know what God wants so that He can bless us.

If you aren't being blessed, then ask God why. Sometimes the problem is in the timing. More often than not, it is because we don't know how to tap into the glory so that we can receive those blessings. We need to step into the river. That river has currents. There is an ebb and flow to the glory.

What does the Lord say to some people when they get to Heaven? He says, "I never knew you" (Matthew 7:23). The people He says this to didn't work with what He gave them. They didn't move in what He poured into them. They didn't use what He had deposited.

You want to use all that God has given you because it's forever. It's forever! Forever means that you can see great distances like the eagle. That's the eye of the Spirit. You just keep seeing. When God gives you a word, it isn't the end of the message. That word is connected to His eternal purposes.

ATMOSPHERE

Kevin here, friends, to tell you about another important element to access the glory realm—*atmosphere*. Many of us are familiar with humbling ourselves with prayer and fasting. We will be touching on these topics shortly. We must always be mindful that we are coming before a Holy God. We can come boldly into the throne room, but that boldness must carry an attitude of humility and holiness.

We are to strip away the lusts of the flesh to a point where the things of the physical world are put to death. Then our spirit can hear and respond to the movements of God. When we do this, we will be at a place of peace. As we allow the Father to touch our heart, we will respond in ways that touch His.

When I was first launched a few years ago, I was launched in the glory. When I went on *Sid Roth* and TBN and began doing the ministry God gave me, I was speaking from the glory, because that's where I came from when I died. So when I came back, I didn't know anything else after it.

Before that, I used to operate in the anointing and the gifting and things like that. But afterward, I talked to someone who is a father to me. I have several fathers. I asked, "Can you tell me what's going on here, because when I start speaking, I feel like the courts of Heaven come to where I'm at? I don't go to the courts of Heaven. They come to me." The father said, "Well, that's because you're speaking from the glory." The man knew Sister Ruth Heflin. He said, "What you're doing, Kevin, is you are speaking from the glory. You've never left. When you came back, you never left the cloud, so it comes with you."

He spent a long time explaining it to me. He understood that there were different areas of the temple. The Old Testament talks about these different areas. There was the outer court, the inner court, and the Holy of Holies. *The Holy of Holies is the glory.* The glory is the place where we enter into the Holy of Holies, and where our Lord is seated on the mercy seat. The atmosphere there is very different than the one we live in, here in the world.

When you enter into the glory, you are in the cloud. When you speak from the glory, it comes with you. It comes when you draw near. The glory, the way of the Lord, is a higher place. Once you enter in, you aren't going to ever want to leave. You will watch over it carefully. You become a protector of the glass. You hide yourself in God and protect what you have. It becomes part of your heart.

When the glory comes, you will sense the winds of the Lord blowing around you. Reach in and take hold. Let God do what He wants to do. Examine yourself to see if you are in faith. We need to have faith in order to please God.

It says that we have to first believe that God exists and that He is a rewarder of those who diligently seek Him (Hebrews 11:6). We need to be sober-minded and discerning. When we discern that God is moving and where, we need to step into that place and move with Him.

We are to move with God. Do you remember that Jesus said that we are to "occupy"? We are to occupy the things that He has called us to do. We aren't supposed to just occupy physical space and sing songs. We are supposed to change the very atmosphere wherever we walk, but we are to do this with humility and holiness. Now let's listen in as Sister Ruth describes the kind of atmosphere that is required to access the glory realm.

(*Sister Ruth now shares.*) Dear friends, we are entering into a new and higher realm that requires a very different atmosphere than what we have known. We are in the hour when God is putting His touches on us at such a height. There is a higher level. Right now, we are only in the middle of the stairway. We are going higher.

He said, "Come to the secret places of the stairs" (Songs 2:14). Come to the secret places. There is a message hidden in this. It talks about *Psalm 91*. That says, "He that is in the secret place of the Lord, that dwelleth." He should say, "*Come in.* He that dwells in the secret place of the Most High, shall abide under the shadow of the Almighty" (Psalm 91:1). Abide in Him. He is calling us to walk with Him and to abide in Him.

Again, the atmosphere we create allows us access to the glory realm. We are helping to create an atmosphere in the physical realm, which brings in the glory when we occupy the things we are called to do.

I have learned that by singing and worshiping, we can actually hear the glory come in. You can hear it! I have heard it coming in like a mighty flood when God was about to bring change. I knew that change was coming. I could feel the pain.

There is an operation in the Spirit that takes place. It's not just a surgery in us. It's an operation to alter how God wants to move in the body. We have to move with the Lord and be ready for the changes that are coming. We aren't to be floundering around. We aren't even swimming. The currents of the heavens will overtake us and carry us if we allow that to happen.

When you learn the ways of the Lord and His moves and timing, you realize that you have to do things right now. God is moving right now. The glory is moving now. It is good to think, "I have to move or I will miss it." I have missed the glory many times because I didn't move in that second when the power of God was ready to be thrust into a situation.

ALTARS

I have told Brother Kevin that I have learned that *altars* are another kind of access point to the glory. Our life is to be laid in the altar. It is to be given unto God. There is to be Kingdom purpose in all that we do. *James 4:8* says, "Draw nigh to God, and he will draw nigh to you." In order to draw near unto Him, we first need to *create an atmosphere* for the glory. It's an atmosphere where God is able to work. Altars are a type of access point that can help us to create an atmosphere of holiness for the glory to come in.

My sister had an experience where she went to Heaven. She had a long visit. Every time she told me about it, I would weep until I could barely see. The Lord first took her to a garden. He said, "Would you like to come and sit in the garden with Me?" There was a bench there. He sat down beside her and began to tell her things. This is what it's all about. God wants to reveal the "now," the future of your life to you.

I made a little altar in my bedroom. I bought a stool and had someone cover it for me. I put it at the end of my bed. I sit there like I am sitting in the garden with the Lord. Build an altar unto the Lord. It doesn't have to be a physical altar. It can be a place where you meet Him, like a prayer closet. Wherever you connect with Him, you are building a place in God, in the Spirit.

There is a certain time in the morning that the Lord expects me. Do you know that He waits for you? I talk to the Lord the way a child talks to their daddy. I say, "I'm here, Lord. I'm here. Lord, I promised You I would be here." Come before Him, excited and expecting Him to do that new thing. Expect Him to share His concerns with you.

A friend told me that one summer, instead of going home from college, he decided to remain at school. He met the Lord at five o'clock every day. He even set an alarm clock in case he became sleepy. The Lord came down from Heaven and said to him, "Do you know how precious this is to Me that you set this time to meet with Me?"

God loves it when we do these kinds of things to honor Him. It causes Him to bring down the glory more quickly as we show ourselves faithful to draw near unto Him. So go ahead and make a set time period in your day to meet with the Lord. Make a little altar or place where you meet with Him. We have to take the time. It literally helps to create a holy atmosphere for the glory of Heaven to come.

PRAYER

I shared with Brother Kevin that when I was a brand-new Christian, God put a hunger in my heart for Him. I had heard and believed that we need *a good prayer life* to know God and to move quickly in Him. That is true. We are to have an active prayer life, including praying in the Spirit.

People don't always feel like praying, but when we begin to pray, what we do soon changes from a physical ritual into a spiritual experience. We can feel the atmosphere change when we open our heart with reverence to the Lord during our prayer time.

He wants us to step into a new level, a greater depth of prayer. Our prayers will be like a river that doesn't just cover our feet. It will cover our eyes, ears, and every part of us. We will be immersed. Our prayer life will baptize us in knowing what God is doing and in what salvation is all about.

It's important to move quickly as there is a set time for things. We need a deeper prayer life today because the Holy Spirit is moving quickly. He will put a demand upon your life. Talk to the Lord about it. That's what I did. I said, "Lord, I want to be used." I prayed for days, "Lord, use me."

My early prayer life was four to six hours a day. I would get up in the morning and the Holy Spirit practically pulled me back into my bedroom. It got to the point where I felt a separation. I was being separated from my old life. When you press in to know the Lord, your prayers are an access point to the glory. You will begin to feel the presence of the Lord and of His holy angels. The atmosphere will change as soon as you begin to pray.

You want to have something to talk about, something to share. You almost want to brag about it. "Look at what the Lord has done in my life." You want to have a wonderful prayer life. Talk to God daily. Spend time in His presence, cut away from the shoreline. Cut yourself away from those things that occupy too much of your time.

Most of the time, I turn off my cell phone or put it away. I don't use it to search out information. I seek God for what He wants me to know. He tells me what is important, what is necessary, and what can be used today.

Your prayer life includes being faithful to the House of God wherever you go. Remain focused on Him. The living creatures in the heavenly throne room keep focused on God, even though they can see to the left and to the right.

Sometimes our words, thoughts, and other things we do don't seem to work. That's because they must be activated. The glory activates you. We must be focused on God in all that we do. He wants us to remove all of the distractions in our life so we focus only on Him, regardless of what is happening in the world.

FIRSTFRUITS

Dear friends, it's Kevin again. Sister Ruth and I both know that we need to put everything aside and give the Lord our morning *Firstfruits*. Before you begin your day, spend time in prayer with Him. Don't say, "I'll do it later," because you will never catch up.

The Lord has said that when trouble comes, we can't go back. Your day and your steps are ordered.

God loves to be the first to meet us in the morning. He wants that time first. He wants to have a conversation with you to instruct you and give you directions. He wants to lay your day out for you so that it is profitable and full of the increase of His ways. If you allow Him your time, you will find yourself laughing and crying at the same time because orders have been sent from Heaven.

God comes from His place to your place just to share His thoughts and His love. Your set times become sacred. You will find yourself wanting to meet with Him earlier and earlier as you come to know Him through His touches in the glory.

Consecrate your time to give God your Firstfruits, the first thing every morning, and He will give you the best gifts. He wants to give you much more than you have asked. His gifts never wear out and they don't cost you, because His anointing is upon them.

God teaches us not to get involved with what we see on television and to keep ourselves separated unto Him. It is so important to *separate* ourselves from the world if we want to enter into the glory realm. God also teaches us never to move in the Spirit and then begin to talk about food, clothing, or how "this was pretty" or "that was cool." Those are the mundane things of life. The Lord has told me several times not to do things to hinder Him from working. Another key factor to walking in the glory realm that the Lord has showed us concerns *fasting*.

FASTING

Fasting is another key access point. It's an important way to humble ourselves and to quickly obtain access to the glory realm. God wants us to release the glory everywhere we go. He wants to be made known in the hearts of everyone. Fasting, reading the Word, and prayer are like the threefold cord that we read about in *Ecclesiastes 4:12.*

Fasting isn't something that people talk about very often, even in the church, and yet fasting breaks yokes! It makes all the difference. It's a catalyst for the glory. You become extremely sensitive to hearing the voice of the Lord when you fast. Fasting turns your attention toward Him and away from your outside interests. Let's turn our attention now to hear Sister Ruth's thoughts about fasting.

(*Sister Ruth now shares more of her story.*) Saints, every word that Jesus speaks is like light or electricity. There is life in it! It's our spiritual food. He is our provision and we have to pursue Him to receive life, and life more abundantly (John 10:10).

Once when my finances were low, I went after the Lord. He didn't tell me anything, even though I pursued Him for six months. At times, it felt like I was paralyzed. When He finally spoke, He said, "The answer you are looking for is in this book, this chapter, and this verse." Well, could He have been any clearer? I wasn't eating of His Word. I was fasting from the Word. You don't want to do that. His Word is life. He said, "I am the way, the truth and the life" (John 14:6).

I tried to convey this to my two nephews. When they were little, I taught them the Bible and how to fast for three days, just on water. Now, that sounds cruel, doesn't it? They nearly fainted, but they saw the Lord in His royal robes. They began to prophesy when they were just ten and twelve. They were new on the block, but they began to see visions.

One of the boys had said, "Aunt Ruth, I don't think I can do it." Today, few people can go three days on just water. Come on! Three days will resurrect you! You will see the glory. We fasted every year in our ministry. Most people did at least a forty-day water fast or a twenty-one- day fast. It was part of our schedule before camp began.

When I was saved for only about a year and a half, the Lord spoke to me about going to Panama. I didn't even know where that was. I didn't know what kind of weather they had there. You have to study these things sometimes, when you are in agreement with the Lord.

He simply said, "Panama." So, I looked on the map without knowing that year-round the country's weather averaged one hundred degrees. I packed a winter suitcase to go to Panama! I didn't have any contacts. I didn't know anyone, but I had been fasting in order to hear God's voice.

Make your life one of fasting. When you fast, you empty yourself out. Fasting makes it easier to hear the Lord. It makes it simple to know His ways. He isn't simple. You just understand Him more as you become more like Him. All of a sudden, you just know. There is a knowing in your spirit. Knowing comes with the glory. You make room for it when you fast. He tells us in His Word why we must fast and why some things don't happen unless we do.

Fasting brings you to a place of being more sensitive. You are more ready and useful. You want to be useful to the Lord. If you work the combination of prayer, reading the Word, and fasting, it will take you anywhere you want to go in the world. The Word says that a threefold cord is not easily broken.

God will lead you in the paths of righteousness, the righteous ways of the Lord. He will carry you on His chariot throughout the Earth when you come up higher in Him. Seek His face. When you find Him, always remember to say, "Yes, Lord, thank You," and "Amen."

HOLY SCRIPTURE

Saints, it's Kevin again, and we are sharing key access points to the glory realm. We have seen a few already that help to create an atmosphere that attracts the glory. However, we can't forget that the most important one is the *Holy Scriptures*.

Jesus often said, "It is written," but how many people bother to ask, "What is written and where do I find it?" We want to know and can begin to know the Lord by studying His written Word. We can attend church, but we have to take time to turn those Bible pages ourselves in order to learn what God wants to say to us.

Sometimes we forget that the written Word is one of the most important access points to the glory that we have been given. While we wait to hear from the Lord, we should also be searching the Scriptures daily for the answers we seek.

We can see that a key to being ready to move in the glory is to eat of the Word every day. We need to read our Bible daily. Some people want to live on one "meal" a week, usually on the weekend.

Sister Ruth and I both agree that you can't do it. You just can't do it. You won't live. God won't let you. If He has to follow you with His Word, He will make sure you eat of it. His Word is life itself. What we eat or don't eat is important.

Learn of Him. When you read the Word, you are reading about who He is. And because you take the time to study Him, as you read the Holy Spirit will begin to give you revelation through the Word. He will open, expand, and overtake your spirit. If you allow His Spirit to overtake you, He will take you into those realms He has placed in your heart. God puts realms into our heart.

We can read all the stories, like those about Paul, Peter, John, James, Philip, and Stephen. We can learn the apostles in alphabetical order and all of the tribes. It's easy. God will use what we learn. Sister Ruth told me that she learned all of the books in the Bible. Then she learned how many chapters were in each book. Do you know what the Lord did? Here's what she told me.

One evening, she was traveling to Texas when she decided to stop at a church. The pastor said, "Does anybody know all the books in the Bible?" She raised her hand and shared what she knew. God will use what we study and learn. It doesn't matter how small it is. He will use it in our life, in some measure.

We must have that constant association with the Lord and seek His desire in every situation. Seek His will and focus on what He wants you to do. You will do simple and great things.

It doesn't really matter. Once we know His will, we simply obey Him. We go and do.

Jesus told us that we can find all we need in the Word. (Study *John 15:7* and *Second Peter 1:3*.) He was saying, "These are the important things, so put the emphasis on what is important." Focus on Him and you will never fail to walk where He is leading you. The Word is a lamp unto our feet and a light unto our path (Psalm 119:105).

I have learned that we are to pray to step into the river of glory. Pray more in the Spirit, in your supernatural language, in tongues. If you do not yet have the gift of tongues, then be certain to give your life to the Lord and ask Him for this gift.

Tongues are a private, supernatural language that is between you and God. The enemy has no ability to interfere with or operate in a supernatural prayer environment. When we pray and speak and sing in tongues, we are praying great mysteries. We are praying forth our destiny.

It doesn't matter what goes on politically or what you hear about the world. Remain focused on God at all times. Focus on the Lord when you pray. Focus on Him when you read the Word. Focus on Him when you worship. Focus on Him in all that you do.

God will speak to you as you meditate upon His Word. There is life in every word. You make it come alive by reading it, speaking it, and applying it to your life. God is Spirit. He operates in His Word.

Don't fall short of what God wants you to do. Remain in the Word. It's not just about *knowing* the Word. We are to *abide* in the Word until it comes alive in us. We become filled with the presence of the Lord. His words are life, and life more abundantly (John 10:10).

More than ever before, it is critical for every person to know the Lord. Time is short and eternity is approaching. Judgment Day is coming soon. Are we ready to stand before the Lord? We need to ensure that we know Him and that He knows us. We don't want to hear, "I never knew you" (Matthew 7:23).

There are doors that God will open. He will absolutely astound you. He has a purpose for you in His heart. You will be so amazed. He will thrill you with the way He works. He said, "These things will be added to you, if you seek Him" (Matthew 6:33). If you seek what He wants and what pleases Him, you will be busy night and day, doing the Lord's work until He comes.

Acquaint yourself with God in the usual ways and in new and unusual ways. Go after Him. Wait upon Him. Ask Him something you don't understand and let Him work it out in your spirit. Be the testimony of who He wants you to be. You want to have a testimony. The Word is God's testimony.

In the beginning was the Word. The Word was with God, and the Word was God (John 1:1). If you want to know where you are supposed to be going, it's helpful to look back "in the beginning" so that you can begin anew. It is only when we humble ourselves and pray that God says that He will hear from Heaven (2 Chronicles 7:14). When you draw near to Him (especially in His Word), He will draw near to you through the glory realm.

HEAR AND OBEY

(*Sister Ruth is now speaking.*) God wants to share His thoughts with us. He said, "My thoughts are without number" (Psalm 139:17-18). That means we can't count the thoughts of the Lord. He said, "My ways are past finding out" (Romans 11:33). We'll never be able to write them down in this Earth.

Ask Him anyway and wait until He tells you the answers. Keep asking. He will talk to you. Tell the Lord, "I'm ready to hear what You have to say. Lord, I promise You." We can be so carnal, fleshly. We have to promise the Lord that we won't get upset with Him when He wants to tell us something.

Then *prepare* yourself. You have to prepare all of the little places. There is a lot of "little" inside of you, like little clefs that have to be opened. Do you know how there are clefs in music? Those clefs have to be opened so that someone can hear. God is trying to speak revelation to us. We hear it with our flesh, in our natural language, but He wants us to have a deeper level of knowing in our spirit. He speaks to us in our spirit.

WAIT UPON THE LORD

The Lord once told me, "You've learned of My ways and you've learned of My dealings." That doesn't mean that I know everything, but when you go to the woodshed enough times, you decide not to go there anymore. Learn the Lord's ways and His dealings. Learn your lessons the very first time.

You want to listen to what God is saying to you so you can learn of His ways. He said, "My ways are high and your thoughts are not Mine. I want you to know My thoughts" (Isaiah 55:9). They are so precious. They are wonderful and full of glory. I wanted to know, so I began to ask questions.

Sometimes we must wait a while after we have asked the Lord what it is that He wants us to do. Even when I see an obvious doorway opening that I believe I may enter, I *wait* for the Lord to explain to me exactly what I am seeing. How many times have you seen things and waited for the Lord to explain them to you? We need to learn how to *wait on the Lord*. There is a proper, divine timing.

God puts me aside for a few months so I can build myself up in the Spirit. I do this by praying in the Spirit, listening to hear the Lord, and by being obedient to Him. When I first began to do this, I sometimes thought, *Am I really hearing Him?* I knew it wasn't the enemy. It was a spiritual thing that was just new to me.

The Bible says, "It is good for me to draw near to God: I have put my trust in the Lord God, that I may declare all thy works" (Psalm 73:28 KJV). We need to draw near to God in order to enjoy the benefits of a close relationship. Most people are as close to God as they want to be. They don't know the benefits of desiring more. They don't know that they need to change their mind about some things.

I admit that at times, I have felt cold. It was as if I wasn't hearing anything. I would ask, "Lord, are You still there?" You start searching. You really can't ask anyone about it because God is asking you to come closer to Him. There may be hesitancy in your spirit, but don't resist.

We will have to change our schedules and even our way of giving. We will change the way we pray. We will talk less and listen more as we *wait upon the Lord*. We are to wait upon Him.

I humbled myself under the mighty hand of God until He exalted me. Before God promoted me, I felt like I was backing up. It's a process. If you want to fly, you have to first learn how to walk and then run. We don't skip steps.

Once the glory comes, you may wonder how you are to keep it or maintain it. You have to move with the cloud. Stay in the cloud, in the hidden place. The enemy will try to distract you. Be diligent.

God has given us knowledge. He speaks to us. We have to use it. It's part of our inheritance. We aren't to spend it on everything. Know where to apply it to get the interest back on what God has given you. (See the parable of the talents in *Matthew 25:14-30*.)

The Word says, "Learn of Me." Learn about Him. Learn about His ways. Then learn who He is. You will feel His constant presence when you start learning what really pleases Him.

I found out that I had to allow God to subdue me. I had to do things I didn't want to do—things that weren't in my nature. I had to do things that I had thought I didn't need to do. Let God have His way with you. Don't make excuses why you don't want to go where He is leading you.

There are times when we must wait on the Lord. Right now, we are in the days of Elijah. There is this element of hurrying. Often there isn't time to pack a suitcase or get things ready. Sometimes God gives you only a moment's notice. He will say, "Go here. Go there." I learned that Elijah couldn't take much with him. He said, "You go there and wait."

When I get in the Spirit, I'm not mindful of people. I have been places where I didn't realize that people were watching me. I don't think, *What am I doing?* I'm singing unto the Lord! People see me talking. They think maybe there's a little something wrong upstairs (in my mind). No, it's being made right!

Often, I will ask questions of others before they get a chance to ask me. I'm bold enough to do it. I say, "I'm talking to the Lord. Have you done it today?" I don't worry too much about what other people think about me.

If we want to see the goodness of God, we will let Him do the pruning He wants to do. Let Him remove what offends His purposes and what limits Him from working in your life. You won't be waiting forever. You will be at the front of the line!

Wisdom says, "Hold off and wait on the Lord. Don't always judge things according to your mind." That's because you might miss what is really going on in a situation. We need to look to the Lord and then use wisdom in the waiting. When He tells us to wait, we wait until He tells us to move. When He says it's time to move, then we are to obey and not make excuses.

I don't find myself admiring a lot of things that are trendy. I don't go after them. I don't watch too much television. The Lord told me that this is where the trouble began. He said, "I don't want you to get caught up in the news." It's a distraction.

He told me, "You have to let your mind be free." No matter what is happening, you are above. We are part of that great eagle. We are to soar into those higher realms. The Spirit always sees what we cannot. When the Spirit comes, it's like a key that opens you up.

When I was staying at a friend's house to help with something, I heard a song in my spirit. The words were "life seconds numbering." Life seconds were being numbered. I didn't know that the song was meant for my sister-in-law. God had told me to go and minister to her. I stayed with her for six months while she had cancer. It was very difficult. She wanted to sleep all of the time. I didn't know or recognize her symptoms.

She got up one day and we talked about the glory of God. She was looking in the mirror when she said, "Oh, I look just horrible." I said, "Yeah, I know, Shirley, look at me." I didn't have the understanding I have today. I was giving her all of these reasons and comparing things in the wrong way. Sometimes we agree with others to make them feel better. Don't do that. Give people words of *inspiration*.

Shirley told me she never wanted to speak in "those tongues." She asked me, "Do you speak in a funny language?" A funny language! I said to her, "Like this?" I began to sing in tongues. She said, "Yes. What is that?" I told her what I knew.

She had two boys who were ten and twelve at the time. While I stayed with the family, I would teach the boys the Bible after they got home from school. One evening, the older boy, who was filled with the Holy Spirit, said something from another room. I didn't catch what it was, but his mother did.

Then he walked into the room where I sat with his mother. Suddenly, he began to speak as if he was a giant from another world. The first words out of his mouth dealt with the conversation the two of us women had shared in front of the mirror, earlier in the day when he and his brother were still at school.

That child took his mother's hands in his and called her by her first name, the way a man would. He said, "Shirley, you are not ugly." Then he turned his face toward me. Still holding his mother's hands, he said, "Ruth, none of my servants are ugly." His words put the fear of the Lord in me!

HEAR GOD'S WHISPERS

God began speaking out of the mouths of those children and giving us daily direction. At one point, our electricity was turned off because someone who had been helping us suddenly deserted us. Something happened and the person paying the bills didn't understand, so they left. But God never left us. He impressed a neighbor to ask us, "Would you like to come to my house each day for a buffet dinner at evening time?" God opened a window of Heaven at the moment of our need and began to take care of us. The provision of the Lord is wonderful.

If you listen for His voice, the Lord will tell you things you know not of! Praise God. This may not seem important, but we have to hear His *whispers*. Know that God is there. He is hiding in the shadows waiting for you and He wants to come out!

You will hear the whispers of God in your daily life and even more so in your prayer life. It's important to lay a foundation that God can build upon. You need a foundation so He can use you. If there isn't much of a prayer life, there won't be much activity. You won't see prophetically. You won't hear His voice.

Another access point to the glory is our *obedience*. We don't want to have a deaf ear, an itching ear, or just a listening ear. That is too many ears. You want to have a hearing ear. The Lord is looking for obedient people.

Do what He tells you to do when He drops something into your heart. Follow the instructions that He gives. It doesn't make any difference if He sends you out to minister to someone and you are in your work clothes. Be obedient to the Lord. Don't wait days or months to do what He tells you to do. If you think about it too long, you won't do it.

I asked Jesus one day, "What did You say that made the disciples follow You?" I am interested in the things that you never hear about. I don't know if the Lord gets tired of hearing my questions or not. He just answers them. It's not childish to ask. It's childlike. We are to become like little children. I prayed my questions for six months. "Lord, I don't really know why I'm asking You this. They obeyed You. I want to know what You said to the disciples. What was the key?"

We all want to obey the Lord. However, at first, the disciples didn't know the Lord. They saw Him and merely sensed something different. Do you know that the disciples weren't all fishermen? Only a few of them were. Study the Word and the history. They came from all different backgrounds, just like we do.

The Lord answered me with three words, like a threefold cord. I heard His audible voice. He has the most romantic voice I have ever heard. It pulled me up out of a deep sleep. The Lord told me the same thing He told His disciples. He said, "You must hurry."

That's what the disciples heard when He said "Come." It's also what they heard when He said "Go." He was saying, "Pray. Accelerate." There is a time frame to the glory. Eternal salvation is at stake.

When the Lord told me to "hurry," I saw my whole life in those words. They went through every part of my spirit like oil. I could feel myself being sealed.

One morning, I woke up several times. I knew I needed something. I started saying, "Lord, I need. I need. I need." He said to me, "You need to put three dresses in a suitcase and go up to Jerusalem—one for yesterday, today, and forever." That "forever" is our tomorrow. This is part of the threefold cord in *Ecclesiastes 4:12*. We need to prepare. We need to hear from the Lord and we need to be obedient.

The Lord spoke to me, but I waffled. I asked, "Are those the dresses for coming and going?" We are always looking for reasons why we need to do something. I don't remember the Lord carrying a big suitcase anywhere! We know so little about His apparel. We only know that He leaves and returns with another wave of glory upon people's lives.

I find that we shouldn't try to have our own way in front of God. Let Him speak. He knows the end from the beginning and all that is happening. Over time, we will see the inner workings of all that He is doing.

When you disciple, don't take more than you need to. Everywhere I go, I tell people, "Don't heap burdens upon yourself. Get your dress for yesterday, today, and tomorrow." That's the resurrection, right there. I know that some women are thinking about that. Don't get involved with trivial things or unnecessary conversations.

God will have exactly what you need when you need it. If He wants you to have it, He will find it and bring it to you. Praise God. He knows how to do it with the greatest of ease. The glory brings the *ease* into your life. You learn to adapt to it until it becomes a lifestyle. I want to walk in the lifestyle of Heaven. Don't you? It's having exactly what you need, praise God.

While I was staying with my sister-in-law and her family, she went into financial hardship. God told me, "Money is coming in the mail." My sister-in-law received something that she thought was a notice or an advertisement, so she tore it in half. She had never heard the voice of the Lord before that day. She threw the mail into the trash. Suddenly, she heard a voice say, "Go back and get that out of the trash can."

When she obeyed, she found that she had torn up a check for one hundred and thirty-five dollars. Now, that's when things weren't very expensive. It was enough money to turn her lights back on, turn the phone back on, buy food, and put gas in the car. The Lord also told her, "Take the remaining money and buy yourself an outfit to wear to church." He told her exactly what to buy. The Word tells us that obedience is better than sacrifice (1 Samuel 15:22). God is looking for people who say, "It is no longer I but You that live in me" (Galatians 2:20). It's You working here. Amen?

One day I chose to obey a person of God rather than God Himself. My disobedience blew the electricity out of the church. All of the cameras and microphones went out. It happened because someone wanted me to change the order and flow of the service. It was a big deal.

A well-known Christian band had been invited to be part of our service. I said, "I don't think we should do that. I think it's launched to do what God wants." I said to the person three times, "I don't really want to do that." I kept saying, "I'm telling you, I don't want to do that." Well, God isn't going to arrest the other person. He is going to arrest me because I obeyed the flesh and not the Spirit.

Finally, after four times of saying that I didn't want to do it, I said, "Okay." I knew I was in trouble when I said it. Listen. You don't want to be in trouble when you follow God, and you don't want to know much but not use it.

The church people wanted to take things to another level. They wanted more vision and more time. But as soon as I picked up the microphone, all of the electricity blew out the sound system, yet the lights stayed on. It was strange. I just put the microphone down. For the rest of the evening, my body trembled.

When I went to bed that night, I knew that God was going to speak to me. You will know when you have done something against the Lord. I had a knowing that He was going to speak to me. Once before, He had spoken to me about something I had done. I remember telling Him, "You'll never have to chastise me on that again."

Well, that night I was asleep for about two minutes. Suddenly, it felt like my finger had been put into a socket. I was shocked by the power of the Lord as I heard these words, "Strange fire." What was done in the service wasn't what the Lord had wanted.

God is very good to us today, even though we have strange fire in the churches. Many people aren't allowing the Holy Spirit to carry the church into a place of wonderful change.

I have made mistakes that have ruined the purposes of God when I acted too soon. I simply learned not to do that. You will learn from your mistakes. God leads us and teaches us how to walk in the supernatural.

You want to be at the place where you can hear God speak clearly. You won't just let what He says go on by you because of His mercy. If you do, you'll make that mistake again. Learn your lessons once and keep moving forward.

We have to surrender our will daily. Some mornings, the Lord tells me what clothes to wear. I just see a flash, a vision of it. When you travel through life, don't bring a suitcase full of ideas. Travel light. Have the mind of the Lord and what He wants to do and you will travel far.

(*Kevin now shares his thoughts.*) Friends, God has to do things His way. There is a time of preparation. We are like children in school. We have to be prepared for the next grade and the next. Each level requires more strength, more effort, more time, and more order in our life. The higher we go in God, the more discipline that will come and the more order He is going to require. Discipline is part of God loving us. He is treating us as sons and daughters.

People want the glory, but they don't always realize that it comes with a cost. At times, I felt like I was going backward, but I was actually being promoted. Promotion comes when we put ourselves into a humble position.

Before the glory comes, there is a time of waiting. Waiting upon the Lord is part of a life walking in glory. The key for the next few months is to wait upon the Lord. I hear people talk about waiting. They speak it suddenly and my spirit catches it.

When people wait, it "shall renew their strength" (Isaiah 40:31) so they can go on. We wait to see things that are at a great distance, like the eagle. The Spirit always sees it, so we unite with the Spirit. We are being strengthened as we wait.

Elisha gave excuses why he couldn't go right at the moment Elijah came for him. Elijah didn't let those things enter his mind. He said, "It doesn't have anything to do with me." Sometimes people will say a lot of little things when they are trying to be comfortable. Know when to speak and when not to speak. I have had to learn that.

Wait on the Lord and be comfortable in the waiting. Don't make excuses in order to make yourself feel comfortable. Our attitude toward the Lord has everything to do with our ability to walk in the glory.

I have seen the Lord be a little strict with me. He has said, "I didn't bid you to come." At one point on the sapphire stone,

He said, "Unless I extend My scepter and bid you to come, you cannot come."

You cannot walk on the sapphire stone of the throne room unless you are invited. A level of holiness is required. People today often don't respect, honor, or fear God. These are important aspects of moving in the glory.

God dictates which doors open and which things are available to us. There are things that we need to know, that many people in the body don't know. If we would only move closer to God, in a flash we would know and understand things we didn't, just moments ago.

People think they are waiting on God. He is really waiting on them. The angels of Heaven are ready and willing to bring people into the glory realm if we would only learn how to take the right steps in that direction.

GOD IS WORKING

(*Sister Ruth begins sharing.*) As Brother Kevin has said, we need to know what direction we are to walk. I wasn't told what to do today, but I suddenly felt that I should take a few notes. Take note of what you hear and what is going on around you. The glory is all around, like an ocean. The Word says, "The knowledge of it would be in the Earth, like the ocean" (Isaiah 11:9). What God is doing will be all around you. There will be signs. You won't miss it and you won't lose or lack anything.

God isn't short, nor will you lack learning of His ways. There is never an end to what He tells you to do. He just adds another side of the story. He adds another part to who you are. He builds His name and His fame inside of you.

This is the real King. He is over every other king. He is over everyone. Have you met Him? Do you know Him? Does He know you? God is working. He is in charge and He is way ahead of you. He has all of these plans that aren't always predictable.

If God can trust you to be faithful with what you are given, you will pray prayers and He will answer them before you even ask Him. He will already be working on things. You will have an answer in the same day. When you are quick to respond to His voice, He will be quick to respond to yours.

I remember walking into certain meetings knowing that God was going to heal that day. Other times I knew there was going to be repentance. You can feel behind the scenes much of what is going on. You can feel what the Lord is doing in a room.

Sometimes you have to coach people because they actually resist the Holy Spirit. They are busy. They are on their phones in worship. They bring in trash from the outside world. Their lives have been compromised by the world. People often come into meetings with the wrong thinking or the wrong mindset.

As a minister, you almost want to do things for people. Few are ready to walk into the Holy of Holies. You can't truly enter in without a level of holiness. You have to kind of go back to the outer court and start from there. We want to make ourselves ready before we enter into the Holy of Holies.

I remember asking the Lord, "Is there anybody in this room who can help me to agree? Is there anybody who knows what You want? I know what You want, Lord. You want to come down and visit us and share with us." I wasn't always this confident.

I knew that I wouldn't say "no" to the Lord, but I admit that at times I have dragged my feet a little! When I didn't want to do something, do you know what happened? God would set up another place for me to try again. He would say, "I told you to do this, and this is what I want you to do." He will not force you, but you may wish that He had forced you in the first place!

As Brother Kevin mentioned earlier, there are certain dynamics about our walk with God that the glory can sometimes make you feel certain ways. Know that there is always something more. When you aren't in that place of "more," it can feel like you aren't moving forward but backward.

The Lord reveals that this feeling of immobility or backward movement is just you being in the place where He wants you to be. He is weighing you in the balances. He is determining how well you can be trusted. He wants to give you more and tell you more.

God is moving in the silence. He is telling you, "Leave the old behind. I'm doing a brand-new thing you haven't seen before." You are to get ready. There will be a changing of the mind and a changing of the guard.

The old goes. You don't even want to lean on it. You don't want to look back into it. Your conversation will change. From the day that I came to the Lord, I changed my lifestyle and even my friends. It's like animals that shed their skin. You have to leave the old behind and all that you know. He is teaching you differently. You haven't lost the old. It's still there. God wants to know you in new and different ways.

There is so much to discover with the Lord. When we have been seeking Him for a while, we can go through this kind of lonely period before we encounter the glory realm. Sometimes it can feel a bit like we are in a time of isolation. We may be called away from our friends and family.

(*Kevin shares his thoughts.*) As Sister Ruth has hinted, some people feel like they are in a spiritual holding pattern. They can't move forward but they don't want to go backward. They feel they have entered into a dry season. They are constantly waiting, even when their spirit wants to move forward. This is when we should press in.

There is a time of separation. This separation has purpose. God is waiting to see if you are going to take a step closer to Him. Step closer. At first, we may not understand this change. Then God may say, "Step up a little bit higher. I'm doing something new in you." He is preparing to do something new. That's why this change comes.

Sometimes a person's mind is infested with too many other things. They aren't necessarily sinful things. There can sometimes be things that clutter our mind and life. These are things that aren't part of what the Lord is doing. They don't fit His plan or purpose for our life. We need to cleanse our lives from things that don't serve God before we can move forward.

Even Moses backed into a crevice in that rock (Exodus 33:22). He backed in. Then he saw God's glory. We don't want to say the word "backslide," because that isn't what is happening. You will feel a whole lot of things. You will feel all of that mixture coming out of you. You will feel the crooked becoming straight and the limitations going higher.

Over time, there will be less and less of you and more and more of Him and what He wants to do in your life. You will have to forget what you know. Don't worry. It's still there. It's laid in the foundation.

Here is the dynamic that is at work. You aren't going backward, but you aren't yet moving forward. You are simply standing still and seeing the goodness of God in your life. While you wait, you are to be cleansing and preparing. God is always there. When He isn't talking, He is showing you that He is doing something new. There are times when God will be silent. Sometimes He's very silent. People need to know this because some people think there is something wrong when they don't hear anything.

God's silence isn't an indicator that something is wrong, but we do want to hear His voice and feel that comfort in Him. He will step back so that you can come into a new realm. He does this to see if you will cause yourself to move into it.

It's effortless, but the heart cries out. God is more concerned with our character than our comfort. So get hungry and desperate and things will suddenly happen. The glory will overwhelm you. It's always new, again and again.

In the glory, angels come to visit you as God begins to move in your life. The area around you lights up. In Heaven, people who are lit up can be seen. Angels go back and forth, ministering to them. God is getting them ready for their next phase. Demons can also see those who are lit up. Evil spirits will try to hinder you because they can see that God is moving in your life. They can see the preparation.

This should encourage those who feel they are being hindered or are going backward. Remember that Jesus set His face like flint for Jerusalem. That was His mission. We need that tenacity of knowing our mission and sticking it out. Every great man and woman of God has these characteristics. They have bulldog faith. They are tenacious.

If we change our perspective, it can almost seem like fun when hardship comes. Hardship is a sure sign that breakthrough is coming. For those who are going through something now and you feel like you are going backward, the Lord is telling you, "This is a sign that you are about to break through and have overthrow in your life." The angels will come to minister to you because you are about to be promoted. There are times when the glory departs. You can't seem to hear God's voice. If that happens, then repent, fast, and pray. Go back to the place where you disobeyed or last felt the glory.

Go back to the table where you were being fed. You don't have to physically go back. Just go back there in your heart and meditate on what was going on there. Revisit what the Lord asked you to do, and then do it. If you do, you will begin to hear His voice again and perhaps even more strongly. You will find that what happened was that the cloud went one way and you went another. In the wilderness, the pillar of fire went one way and the people went another way.

So the solution for you is to return to the last place you heard God speak. Ask Him to forgive you for disobeying. Whenever this occurs, you will find that you were disobedient. The Lord doesn't just excuse you. If He asks you to do something, it is because the pillar of fire is leading you that way. Stay with the glory cloud. Stay with the pillar of fire. Wherever God goes, just stay in the fire.

You are actually tied to the body of Christ in an intricate way. When you are disobedient, it hurts everyone else. It's the same way with the cloud. When the cloud moves, you have to move with it. You may not know it, but if you don't move with it, you are actually robbing other people. Let's return to the cloud ourselves, to hear more of Sister Ruth Carneal's testimony about the glory.

(*Sister Ruth now shares.*) Saints, there is a price to pay when we seek the glory. I'm not saying that you are going to suffer. You will, if your flesh gets in the way. You have to cut that flesh away. You have to cut away all of the things that aren't of God.

You have to surrender everything to move in the glory realm. When you are willing to do that, you will find that the Lord gives you everything you need. Some of the things that seemed so important to you before now don't seem all that necessary. How close you come to God depends on the condition of your heart. He is always looking at our heart.

God has shown me that I have left home. My heart isn't at home anymore. I found something to leave home for. My heart isn't wondering what is happening back home. I'm not caught up in that. I have left that behind forever.

There are things you will have to leave behind and some things that you will have to submit to. There are daily sacrifices. It's about being faithful, steadfast, and set apart.

There are layers in us that God has to remove. He said, "Here a little, and there a little" (Isaiah 28:10 KJV). He will speak to us until we suddenly see His workings. We'll see how things connect and move. He will reveal how we are to work in them.

Let God awaken your heart to love Him. You won't even ask for things once you love Him enough. He'll show you what your love is all about and what His love is going to do for you.

We need to be people who move in the glory. Be willing to do whatever He wants. If He wants you to just sit, then do that. My longest meeting ever was eleven hours long! I think we began around lunchtime and closed at midnight. People couldn't even get up. They were glued. There was such a weighty cloud. People felt heavy.

The glory was substantial at some meetings. There was a gold substance in the air. At times it was hard to see. I remember seeing people who were crawling on the floor. The glory was moving. No one wanted to move or they would miss it. It was God's will. He was moving and speaking. Sometimes it sounds like a whisper.

Do you know that you are meant to release the whispers, the way of the heavens, and the will of the Lord into your life? God loves you with an everlasting love. He has an everlasting covenant with you. He said, "Let the knowledge come" (Ephesians 1:17). That's the knowledge of what God is doing.

When we know Him, we will hear His voice when He speaks. His voice and His help are what keep us going. He says, "Surely goodness and mercy shall follow you" (Psalm 23:6). We quote that, but sometimes we don't recognize God's mercy until later.

"Oh, God has helped me." Yes, He has and He does. His help makes us open up to hear His voice.

He will speak to your spirit, especially when you meditate on His Word. Many people separate God's Spirit from His Word. He said, "I am looking for people who worship in Spirit and in truth" (John 4:23). He wants us to *know* Him. Part of knowing God is to fear Him with reverence. It's spending time listening to His voice and loving Him so that when He tells you what to do, you are obedient. You won't make excuses.

We could almost live forever right now, if we could only process these things. We could be raptured! God said that there are things that He is going to do. He will do them. We want to learn how to work with Him so we can fully appreciate who He is and the great price He has paid for us. It's far greater than we can ever imagine.

There would be praise all the time, if people knew how to talk to God, how to enjoy His love, and how to value all that He does. We often take things for granted, even small things. God works way ahead of us to put schedules into place and to make the timing perfect for what He is doing. Trust the Lord and His timing. He is working all of it out according to His plan for your life.

HEART OF GLORY

(*Sister Ruth's story continues.*) My granddaughter said something cute when she was little. She asked, "Nanny, how do I get saved?" I said, "You have to get Him in your heart, honey." She said, "Well, how do I get Him in my heart?" I told her, "You have to open the door."

Well, she was only six, so she looked inside of her blouse to see. Then she said, "I don't see the door, Nanny. I don't see the door." When she said that, she fell on her face in the Spirit. She took it literally. Something in her opened unto the Lord.

When she was still young, she suffered a few things that created rubble around her. In the Spirit, I saw her hand come through that rubble. It was reaching out to God.

Our *hands* are another access point to the glory. Our hands are responsible for many of our works. They can reveal how much we appreciate God. A simple example is when we lift our hands in prayer or worship.

When she was young, the Lord told my granddaughter, "Don't put a Band-Aid over anything. Let Me work. Let Me heal. Let Me bring forth who I AM." She didn't understand it at the time, but God captured her heart and her interest. Now she is studying to know Him more.

When we love the Lord, we will follow Him and study all of the things that He has done for us. There are little seed kernels that must open. I tell people there are seals that God puts into us. They open long enough for us to receive their eternal purposes. Then God closes them back up again.

When you go to a church service, don't get on the phone or involved in conversations. Begin working your faith so God can open up that service for you to enter into with your whole heart. If you do this, you will get everything you came for and more. That's because you have come seeking the Lord. You have come to hear from Him. You want to know Him. The church isn't just a building to you. It's part of the sanctuary and building of God. It's an access point for the glory.

It's good to have fellowship. I understand that. When it's rich, it's valuable. A rich man watches over his valuables, doesn't he? He has insurance for the precious things. We have the assurance of Jesus and that's more than precious. It's priceless. Fellowship and take it all in, seal it up, and take it home.

Our hearts need to be arrested by the glory so that we can know Him and speak from the heart of God. We want to move into another atmosphere. God wants to bring back the works of the early church, like the healing line. I am not against doctors or hospitals, but hands will be laid on the sick and they shall recover. Hands will be laid on you and you will have direction. Hallelujah!

You will be in the atmosphere where God is moving. You will know His movements. You will know His wonderful plans. In the glory realm, there is a knowing. It brings an ease for you to move in. That ease allows you to trust in Him. He is continually guiding you into the things that make your life one of purpose.

These are the jewels of the Kingdom. He said, "When I come to make up My jewels" (Malachi 3:17). You will see the beauty of the Lord and the Spirit of holiness working in you. He says, "Worship Me in the beauty of holiness" (1 Chronicles 16:29). He is saying, "Worship Me for what I have done in your life. Let the beauty be seen."

We only see a little. Do you know that God will show you moments of the way things were before the world began? He will bring eternal moments into your spirit to show you how to walk with Him.

In Jesus' day, people were waving palms and singing songs of victory. Those were the sounds of glory. The glory moves in the sound. We are bringing in the Ark and the gold. That's the gold that God has been working on. He says, "How is it that the fine gold has become dim?" (Lamentations 4:1). Understand that God allows trials and pressures to polish the gold.

When we realize this, we won't be accusing the person we think is causing a problem. It really isn't them (Ephesians 6:12). God is trying to show us the strength to come up to this mountain, this holy place, where we declare who He is.

We are to get to know the Lord. We are all learning to know Him. We can come closer to His heart by using the glory access points. We must also remember to be diligent and to wait upon Him. He says, "They that wait upon the Lord shall renew their strength" (Isaiah 40:31 KJV).

To operate in the glory, we need to be strong in the Spirit. We can't take days off from the Lord, like spiritual vacations. We can't put aside the time we spend with the Lord for other things. You will be glad that you spent that extra time for that extra song He gives you and for His ideas and views that He shares with you. You don't want to miss what He wants to reveal to you.

Do you know how people buy glitzy or sparkly clothes? On some level, they are trying to discover what Heaven looks like. People buy sparklers and shiny things because they want to see something bright and moving. Come on. Jesus is our morning star. Move with Him!

God wants to make men and women "a power and a praise." He wants people to have listening ears and open hearts. He wants to share His thoughts toward us. He said, "My thoughts are many" (Psalm 40:5). Draw nigh to Him and He will draw nigh to you (James 4:8).

The Lord spoke to me when I was young. He said, "Make no plans and prepare not your own way. But put yourself in My hands and I will show you what I can do with you." He was saying, "I'm going to pour My glory on you so that you can release it to other people."

In the beginning, I didn't understand what the glory meant. The glory is *His story*. It's history. It's what God can do, has always done, and will continue to do. Great are the ways of the Lord. They are easily understood when we move into the ease of the glory, the ease of the atmosphere of Heaven.

The Lord says, "I'm doing a new thing" (Isaiah 43:19). It's brand new. He will take all the worries, fears, and even the years (for those who think they are too old). I used to think, *When I'm eighty*. You know, maybe I've been good to my parents that long. He said to be good to our parents, so I prepared my insurance. I prepared everything. I thought, *This is it*. I heard the Lord laugh at that. He said, "Die? You're going to live for Me!"

That's what we want to do. Don't be concerned with age. He's the Ancient of Days! We want to live for the Lord. Live every existing moment for Him. We want to get into the place where we wake up in the morning and each day is new. It's a place of passion where we say, "I can't wait."

The fire will be upon you. He's going to spread fire. It's not going to be just a little fire here and there. He wants to put a flame in your heart to start a fire everywhere you go! It will make people hungry. Your voice will even sound different. Come on, throw a little more of the earthly into the fire and watch God!

Joshua was told, "Tell the people to prepare themselves. You have not been this way before" (Joshua 1). There is going to be a lot of taking off and putting on only what is valuable and what will move the hand of God.

You are going to be dressed to stand before the King. You're like Esther. You're about to save a nation. You're about to save a people. You are about to do what hasn't been seen before, nor has anyone heard about it.

It's going to be so new to you that you will give Him anything because you love Him so much. You'll say, "Lord, what do You want? You can have it. Just take it all, but set me free to do what You have called me to do."

We spend countless, perhaps thousands of hours of vain time, searching for clues how to operate with God, like in this last move or in any revival. Here is another clue. It matters how we introduce ourselves to the Lord. It matters how we approach Him when we pray and when we worship. It's all about *the state of our heart*. We are to be humble before our holy King.

Think about how people approach the kings and queens of the Earth. They almost shake in their spirit. We are to *consider* the Lord before we approach Him. Consider Him in all you do. Pour out to Him. Say His name with such adoration and love. Really reverence Him and He will tell you things you can't even repeat.

Here is an example of considering the Lord. In Arizona, the weather was very hot. A group of us had heard about a prophecy that said that God was going to make hot places cool and cool places hot. We decided to pray that the Lord would bring the temperatures down.

After we had prayed daily for months, we had a nice winter and spring. Whenever we approached the Lord, we said, "Lord, we don't deserve it. We're nothing special. It's hot. *Would You consider?*"

The Bible talks about considering the Lord (2 Timothy 2:7). We asked, "Lord, would You consider adjusting the temperature for us?" Then, for three hours, we just thanked the Lord. "Thank You. Thank You. Thank You!"

We kept talking to the Lord about His consideration and about how much He loves us. We weren't asking for any favors, but *would He consider* making it a little more comfortable for us?

He did. Hallelujah! It was so amazing. All we could do was thank Him every day. It wasn't just once that He made the weather cooler. As more and more cool days went by, we continually thanked Him for His consideration.

He says, "Come before the throne" and "Ascribe greatness unto Him." We need to be grateful for all things, whether they are great or small. When we are grateful, we never lack. You will have what God has promised you and much more. You will see His goodness.

His goodness will create a kind of brokenness inside of you. You will want to help others in the same measure He has given to you, just because He has been so good. He has watched over your concerns. We are to be thankful in all things. Consider how good and how loving the Lord is.

Who can measure the holy city? Who can measure the depth of what God can do? In all your ways, acknowledge Him. Understand Him. Have a praise report and you'll be looking at the next mountain, the next place where He will take you into the depths of His love. He will give you His confidence, His love, His peace, and His joy. We will be joyful and we'll make a joyful noise.

I was raised in the Pentecostal Church. We saw a lot of miracles, but we didn't have the joy. We weren't entertaining the Lord. We are to entertain the Lord. Talk to Him about anything and He will start talking to you. I became like a little child.

One day the Lord said to me, "You are like a child sitting on My lap." I didn't know how to love the Lord. Before that, I was just being used. I had the gifts. Then I realized that it is *relationship, not fellowship* that the Lord really wants from us. He is our Father. He is our husband. He is our very best friend. We can tell Him anything. One day, I just turned my heart over to Him.

You are having a heart-to-heart with God. You are thinking about Him all of the time. You aren't being silly. You have that joy of what the Lord is doing on this journey. You will wonder, "How didn't I see this before? How did I miss this?"

Isaiah 54 talks about how even your offspring will inherit the Earth because you have been obedient to rejoice. He says, "Again,

I say rejoice in the God of your salvation" (Habakkuk 3:18). He wants the rejoicing that no one has ever seen. It was only through ministry that I learned to sing a lot in the Spirit.

The glory brings forth a spirit of excellence. I know you all want that. You want it on your tests. You want it in your business. You certainly want it! The glory brings excellence. It's the revelation of Jesus in the midst of us. We are going to give Him a voice.

We will give Him a voice that is heard in Heaven. We will give Him a voice that's around the throne. We will give Him a voice that speaks of what He is doing. He is doing something new. You want that refreshing every day. You want the newness of what God is doing.

How many times have you been in a store at the end of a line, and a new line opens up? The cashier says, "I will take that person at the end of the line over there." That's an eternal moment. Allow the Lord to give you His eternal moments and be trained by the best to move in the cloud of glory.

I am in my eighties. I have thought that by now, I would have done my all. But I'm finding out that most people have hardly done ten percent of what God has given them to do. Some people give ten percent in their offerings. They give their tithes. That's about all they will give to God.

Do you know that ten percent won't do? He wants one hundred percent of everything! He made you. You are His workmanship of what pleases Him. We want to stand before Him and hear Him say, "Well done." We want to follow what God is doing so we can see results. God gives us His very best gifts.

The Word says, "God so loved the world, that he gave his only begotten Son, that whosoever believeth in him should not perish, but have everlasting life" (John 3:16 KJV). It also says that if God so loved us, we also ought to love one another (1 John 4:11).

We can ask ourselves if we truly love God when we give Him only ten percent (or less). How much do we love one another when we are only willing to give the smallest portions of all we have? Be generous. Love one another.

The Lord has given us all that we have. What we think is ours doesn't really belong to us. Our flesh tells us that it does. Then, when we don't have the things we think we should have, we are desolate and we cry out. That cry comes from our fallen nature.

I shared how I give the Lord a report several times a year. I get a pencil or ink pen and paper and write down all the things I don't like about myself. Believe me, I hear people say that they love themselves. Paul said, "In myself, I don't find any good thing" (Romans 7:18).

I love what God has done, but I don't like that "self" image. I like what is real and what has been carved into me. I like what expresses all that is in the light of the Word and what God is doing. We are to express Him.

We are to be the light of the world, that something different. If we are the light, people will notice. They will say, "There's something about you. What is it?" Do you know what I tell them? I answer, "Are you ready to hear?" They usually say, "Oh, yes!"

I have a lot of friends who know me only in a small measure. The ones who don't really know me will ask me what's going on. Those who know me don't have to ask. They can feel it. You can hear people's thoughts out loud. Yes, you can! Jesus can, too. That happens when you get a hearing ear. Sometimes there are things we don't really want to hear. We may need to hear them.

We are a light that has come into people's lives. The Lord said that we are the lights. We know that we have to pay the electric bill to keep the lights on, but have we given all that God wants?

We read in the Scriptures, "You have not labored with child. For more are the children of the desolate" (Isaiah 54:1). Did you know what it says, right before that? It says, "And cry aloud!" Make a noise. Just make a noise!

We cry out because we need a taste of the Lord. We need His goodness and His peace. The Word says, "Taste and see that the Lord is good" (Psalm 34:8 KJV). We are blessed when we trust in Him. He provides all we need. It begins with His glory. He comes in His glory when we cry out, when we declare, when we pray, and when we make a joyful noise.

I saw Brother Kevin Zadai on a poster. When I looked at his picture I thought, *What a smile! How can I get that smile?* It covered everything. He has tasted of the Lord. A taste is great for us, but we have to make sure to get the glory inside of us and allow it to work the way that Brother Kevin does.

When you taste of the glory, it's written on your face. Tasting of the glory is an inner thing that comes out through our facial expressions. If you walk along the street, you can also see the stress, torment, and turmoil that people are going through. It comes out through the face.

When I see the glory glow on someone's face, I know that the person has been in the workshop of the Lord. I think, *They have been working.* I don't see it very often, but I can be speaking with someone and, all of a sudden, their face lights up. It looks whiter than a white-hot fire. At that moment, they have looked into the knowledge and the workings of the Lord. They have seen it. His presence begins to manifest. This is what is going to happen to many people. We will manifest the Word in us.

What God is doing will be written like character upon the countenance of people's faces. Your face will shine and glow in the Lord as you walk in His newness. It's going to break forth like that bright morning star, the morning sun. You will see and fall in love with Jesus in a whole new way.

It's so new that you won't have time to look for the new things in the world because what was new is already old. It's going to be brand new with the Lord. You can actually feel the level of faith that is in operation. You can see it. It's hot. Do you know how in the summertime, you can see the heat dancing outside? Well, you can see the heat of the prophetic dancing above people's heads.

In the upper room, people heard a noise. When they were in the upper room, they heard and declared what was happening. But when they got outside of the walls, the people of Jerusalem described what they heard as a noise. Those who are closer to God will describe it as what it is. "This is what is happening in the Spirit realm." The people needed the prophet to come by. Now you will have a new prophetic voice.

(*Kevin now shares his thoughts.*) Saints, we are to *live in the testimony of Jesus.* That's the spirit of knowing. He said, "The testimony of the Lord is sure, making wise the simple" (Psalm 19:7 KJV). You are to be the testimony of Jesus. Walk in the glory.

Walk in the joy of the Lord. Declare what God is doing inside of you, and watch how He will change everyone and everything you touch.

This is the time of the knowledge of the Lord. We can read about the knowledge of His glory in *Habakkuk 2:14*. The knowledge of the glory is the presence and the moves of what God is doing. We are living in that time. Once we understand how this Scripture fits today, we will feel a floodgate open inside of us.

It says, "For the Earth shall be filled with the knowledge." Sister Ruth told me that she felt a river go into every part of her spirit. It says that it shall be *filled*. Say these words: "Fill me Lord, right now. Fill me Lord, with the knowledge of the glory of the Lord, and let me move with it. Let me have my part!"

We're going to be at a loss for words at the awesome, extraordinary, and unusual exploits in our life. Walk by faith in the Lord. His Word never changes. He isn't going to disappoint you, so praise Him. Consider Him. Love on Him. Be established in Him. He has told us that we are made of dust, so we know that He can make something out of nothing. Trust in Him and be glad.

Allow God to mentor you. He does more for those who come closer. The closer you come to Him, the more quickly your prayers will be answered. The working of miracles will take place in your life. He will prove you when you think that nothing is working.

We need to learn how to become givers by nature. That will require a change of heart. If it's work for us to give, we have a heart issue. We want to be transformed by the Holy Spirit so that all we do becomes a labor of love. We are laboring for the Kingdom because we have our Father's eternal heart of love.

Three

MOVEMENTS OF GLORY

Hallelujah! I see people coming in one way, hardly put together, but they are walking out fully filled with the presence of the Lord. I'm speaking from the courts of Heaven. The Lord says, "Come in. It's easy." Come into His gates with thanksgiving. Enter His courts with praise. Praise Him and speak unto Him what He wants to hear. He's in your arena right now. This is where the Lord is at home.

When you praise Him, you begin to hear what He is saying and see what He is doing. You have been dancing, expressing unto the Lord with your feet and hands. You are releasing what God has for your life. Come in with the joy of the rewards of what God has done. Let the joy of the Lord be our strength. God, let our hearts be in tune. Let there be a praise of joy, a declaration such as we've never experienced before, because we love You and bless You Lord. Amen.

—SISTER RUTH CARNEAL

GLORY OF WORSHIP

Sister Ruth here, Saints. Do you know that God loves worship? He said, "I love the gates of Zion more than all the dwellings in Jacob" (Psalm 87:2). God loves to plow our hearts. He wants to plow, to turn the soil over in us so that He can do new things in us. He plows us by speaking to our heart. Recently, the Lord told me that I should share details about worship, praise, and moving into our place in this last-day revival, this last-day reckoning and movement of God. I know it is your desire to walk in this.

Many people do not understand that *worship is the key to the glory realm.* The Lord told me that *worship creates an atmosphere in which Jesus can work.* Worship gives us access. Through worship, God reveals what He likes and what brings the release of His power. God loves our worship. He wants us to celebrate Him and He wants to reveal more of His nature and character to us.

There is a great emphasis on worship today, but man's worship is a different sound than what is found in the glory realm. Through worship, the Lord taught me how to worship Him in the Spirit. The Spirit has a very different sound. Many times it sounds like a tornado.

True worship isn't something where we can say, "Oh, this is a wonderful song," or "I've heard this," or "This is what is happening." It's new. It's a new song, even when it's an old song. God is doing something brand new. They are new songs.

God works in the patterns of our heart. He works in the worship that we give to Him *from our heart.* He has a pattern that

He wants to bring down from the heavens. It will bring us into a new place of learning.

We speak so casually about worship. We see it all over the world and in churches everywhere. Everyone is coming to worship. People are gathering together. Bringing this revival in is going to be two-thirds of the hour that we are living in.

We will be in worship, singing the song of the Lord unto Him. We will sing about what God is doing. Let the song of the Lord be your delight to God. Let your voice declare the revival. Revive what is in you and around you. Whistle if you have to!

We want to be true worshipers. True worshipers experience Jesus. You don't just go in and out of a service and say, "Wasn't that sound wonderful?" You want to be asking what God was doing while you were there. You want to know what God was revealing. What was He releasing to His people? What was He saying to you?

We don't want to have an entertainment mentality, to be entertained. The question to ask ourselves is this: Do we want a relationship? That's what God desires for us to have with Him.

God and His plans are bigger than we realize. We have only ever touched the surface. In the days ahead, He is diving deeper into the pockets of our lives. He is cleaning and cleansing us. Many times this will reduce you to a pool of tears. You are broken inside. You will pour out. All you can do is worship Him. God wants you to pour out. When you do, you will enter into the joy of the Lord.

He is going to come with greatness that we have never experienced. We say that the Lord is great and greatly to be praised. Did you know that we have seeds of His greatness in us? Greatness isn't something we practice. It's already inside of us. We are meant to let it out. It comes from what is in our heart. When we cry out with our whole heart, God answers and the glory comes.

You want to go to a lively church. You want a church that is alive. They aren't just trying to find a song. They already know the song of the Lord and they are singing it unto Him. People who know the Lord will almost always get a new song just as they step onto the platform. It won't be canned or rehearsed until it's worn out.

It will be so fresh that you will say, "Give me another glass. Come on. Let's go swimming in this water. Let's go deeper in this water. Let's move with God, with flavor." We will move with joy. It's not just splashing around on the shoreline. We will go out into the deep.

You can see what God is doing in the world through your songs. The glory falls upon songs. You will feel the glory in the songs. If the Lord is working in one song, then that is where He is working. Sing that song with all your heart!

When you leave the presence of the Lord, you will know it. You will feel as if you are suddenly hanging around on the outside. You won't know what to do. You may think, *What happened? What happened to the service?* But when the glory comes, you will start yelling and making noise. Your voice is your weapon. Use it to declare the glory of the Lord.

You will feel the fire burning inside of you. It is one way that the Lord speaks to you. Everyone has a unique way that God speaks to them. He speaks according to who you are and where you are in Him.

When I traveled with Sister Ruth Heflin, I learned how to be receptive to get the new song, the songs from the glory realm. We had the sheet music from all of the choruses, but that wasn't everything God wanted to do. Part of those songs had been birthed earlier. As I said, songs that we already know will be made new, again and again.

Every hallelujah you say and sing will be new. You will feel the glory coming upon those "Hallelujahs." And you will say, "Say it again!" They will move you. You will feel the glory coming upon them as you sing.

When you taste of the Lord in the glory, it will work its way into the river of God that is in your belly. He told us there is a river there. He says, "The streams thereof make glad" (Psalm 46:4). That river has many outlets. It has tributaries that flow when you worship the Lord.

You don't really know what you are saying, but you give God a place to work when you worship. He will give you a revelation of what you are doing. Believe it or not, you are singing revelation. You aren't just singing a song to tickle ears or cause hair to stand up on people's arms.

Your worship causes the living God to stand up inside of you and in all those who hear your song. What we sing is declaring the wonderful works of God. It's a realm of revelation where God is working.

When we worship, we are walking, speaking, and learning, all at the same time. He is doing all that He wants to do in just a moment. God works quickly. If we can catch that in our spirit, we will move in the flashes of lightnings and the sounds of His thunder all of the time.

The glory can come through even in things that we hear on the news. We will begin to ask, "What is God doing? What is happening in what we hear? Jesus is coming soon!" We should all be shouting, dancing, and clapping our hands before the Lord.

Clapping your hands brings a release. Lifting your hands is a victory sign. It is reaching and receiving. It is a sign that you are totally surrendered to the Lord. We don't realize it, but our worship expresses God's commands and what He wants to do in the Earth.

Do you know that the church seems to come in and go out the same way? It's like a revolving door. It doesn't feel nice to say that, but I want to go to the next door. I don't want to go in and come out the same way.

I want to be changed. I want this personality to change. I saw all of these feet in a vision. It was like a round perimeter above me, like a glass lid on a glass jar. I saw all of these feet that were dancing all around. We want to express what is in the heaven-lies, to bring it into the Earth because He's creating us to be more like Him.

I didn't realize this at first, but we might abandon our thoughts on how church should be "done." Think about how right in the middle of the word "church" are the letters "u-r." You are. You are the church.

When we sing, dance, and clap our hands before the Lord, we are releasing *breakthrough*. Worship is one of the quickest ways to do this. We've been trying to find a formula for breakthrough and how to get what we want.

One day, the Lord said to me, "I want My people to be grateful for what I did for them." You will find yourself dancing, being silly, being foolish, and just clapping your hands. When someone asks you, "What are you doing?" say, "I don't know. I just feel happy inside." You are responding to the Lord and you aren't ashamed or bashful. These are little hints or keys that the Lord as shown me.

WORSHIP ALWAYS RELEASES BREAKTHROUGHS

Just please the King! Hallelujah? Learn to please the King! Delight yourself in the Lord! He said, "I will give you your heart's desire" (Psalm 37:4). Open your heart unto the Lord. He will show you things you don't understand. He will give you wisdom, strength, and a peace only He can provide.

I always had a little song, a little sound inside of me. It was years before I learned how to truly worship the Lord. We sing with our lips because God makes the fruit of the lips. Most of the time, we sing with our talent or from what we know or have studied or practiced. You can't practice God!

One day, I realized that it wasn't just my voice or talent that mattered, even though I came from a family of singers and musicians. God was trying to tell me what was happening in the heavens and I tapped into it. There is a heavenly rhythm. There is a current in the heavens.

When you are near water, you can smell it. You can hear the sounds and see and feel the movements. God wants us to have that triple, full measure in our lives. He wants us to feel, hear, and know what He is doing. We are to delight ourselves as a little child that claps his hands. We are about to get the ice cream of our life.

God wants you to taste of Him. He is without measure. Taste of Him and know that He is good in whatever is happening around you. I feel His goodness even now. I hear the sound of the water spouts. I know the glory of His voice. I see the beauty of His face. He is expressing what He has done and how happy He is.

He is gloriously happy today that you have come to hear and to know that Jesus is more real than you have understood all of your life. He is *real*. He is the best friend and the best partner. He is the best of everything, and that really means *everything,* so put Him first.

Know that you are always going to send Judah first. You are going to declare the coming of the Lord and His greatness. This is what worship is truly about. You are bringing Heaven down. The carpet is there and the King is about to make His entrance.

God wants you to know Him. He will cloister you to study Him and to know Him. There is so much more to know. It won't be the same worship that we have known. He dresses it up a little more. He puts hands and feet and sight on it. He puts ears on it so you can hear what He is doing. He says, "Not only do I want you to sing. I want you to *break forth* into singing."

This means that you are to sing from your heart. That will draw His glory, which will manifest His power. That is true worship. Singing isn't lip service or movement without power. Let God create His fruit in you. The song of the Lord is part of His Word. It comes from Him and it goes back to Him. He is always fruitful and He multiplies.

God is making you a garden of His love. He is making you who He wants you to be. He will tell you all that He is going to do. That is, if you will truly worship Him in Spirit and in truth.

Don't you love it? God tells you exactly how to worship. He tells you how to do things and He tells you what will happen as He shows you how things work. All you have to do is read it, love it, and do it. That's simple, isn't it? He says, "Sing unto him, sing psalms unto him: talk ye of all his wondrous works" (Psalm 105:2 KJV). Sing!

We are to go to the table with a heart and mind of worship. We are going to the table to ravish everything at a divine buffet. Eat the Word. Worship in His presence. Worship His holy name. Worship the God of all flesh. Learn to know Him and worship Him!

Sometimes in our worship services, the Lord will tell me it is time to dance or time to get the tambourine or the flags out or it's time to dance on the Sea of Glass. In meetings, I have suddenly said, "We've got to dance on the Sea of Glass right now," and "The glory just broke wide open."

At first it's in the flesh. But then something will catch you by surprise in the services. You will think, *What is this?* It seems like the streets of Jerusalem or something. There is music and dancing. All of a sudden, you find yourself in the Spirit, but it began in the flesh.

At first, you are just performing. Then after a while, you start to feel something happen in the Spirit. Something is breaking. All of a sudden, everyone is up and out of their seats. They are doing a "Jericho march" around the room. They are dancing and twirling.

It just goes to the next level. Then you speak or whoever the speaker was would get up. I have been part of that where it just goes to another level. We want this. We want to keep going higher. The Lord ordained that.

He almost commanded me to hold a prayer meeting. He said, "Keep the heavens open. Let the glory come." The glory will change people faster than anything else. His presence does that. An anointing ministers to us, but the glory changes us in a way that is an eternal change.

We must always be mindful of the glory. Sometimes we may have to pray when we don't feel like praying. It begins as a physical thing, but then it becomes spiritual. There is a kind of transference.

I appreciate that Brother Kevin has said, "Don't ignore and don't forget and don't give up." I have found that if you have to separate yourself from people, then take care of that because God moves quickly. The glory comes quickly. It's like lightning. You see it here and then you see it over there. You have to catch it.

This glory has come upon me in our services. I recognize when I go into a place that is dry. We don't like to say that. It's very dry. We wonder if God is speaking in that place, but it's so obvious.

People—who have seen Him or who have caught the vision or they know there is more—want it. They are willing to go after it, like the pastor of the church I was going to. He said that if you don't put anything in that microphone, the people aren't going to receive anything out there. The pastor was concerned if he didn't hear from Heaven during the service. He would ask if we were hearing so that we could speak about what God was doing, into the hearts and lives of the people.

When the glory comes, it really fine-tunes your listening ear. That was happening to me. You know something is there and you just want to tap into it. I was learning more and more, but there was still a little place that I could get into. One day, I heard the Lord clearly tell me, "Well, why don't you just tap into it?" I heard His voice, just like that. It was easy.

I didn't really think about the word. I just thought, *Okay, I'll do it.* So now that I had a prayer meeting of my own, what was I going to do for worship? It just hit me. Tap. It's a rhythm. It's the rhythm of Heaven.

I can play a little on a lot of instruments. My family was full of singers and musicians on the keyboards and violin. My mother played accordions and the organ. I wanted to play piano, but it just didn't come through my fingers.

One day, our service had to change because the pianist didn't show up. The man on the drums could play the piano, so he sat there. Believe it or not, I felt those drums calling me. They were saying, "You, come over here." I kept looking at them. I thought,

I don't want to mess up the music. The man on the piano said, "Just do it." I heard him say, "Don't think about it. Just do it." The rhythm and timing just went into my hands. It was the first time I had ever played for rhythms and timing.

About fifteen years ago, I ended up at a revival meeting at a Mennonite church. I was the speaker and was dressed to speak, but someone volunteered me to play the drums because the drummer hadn't shown up. That drum beat would be the key to the whole revival. I didn't hesitate to play. I just said, "Lord, here goes. You are either with me or not!"

There were people there who didn't understand Pentecost. So what do you think happened when a woman got on the drums? The Spirit of God moved around the room! I saw people trying to get out of the hands of the Lord. As we sung, a Mennonite woman pulled the hat off of her head. Then she pulled her hair down and twirled all over the room!

You have to know how God wants to work with people. I was trying to break through because I knew we were in a different atmosphere and with different people. The pastor was sitting over in a corner. There was fire going all around the room. It looked like flames of fire were dropping off of him. He was sitting there watching.

The pastor told me later that he had said to himself, *Lord, I sure hope this is revival!* He was going badly. He was trying to get someone to help him. He was trying to come out of the fire. You should have seen his eyes! Revival was bursting forth in a Mennonite community. It was way out of the people's comfort zones.

SEND THE FIRE

(Kevin now shares his thoughts and describes what was taking place during the interview with Sister Ruth where she described the Mennonite Revival and how holy fire arrived.) Friends, as we have said, there is a Sea of Glass in Heaven, and we need to be mindful of spiritual things. For example, during the interview with Sister Ruth, I was seeing the throne. There were angels that were literally falling down. All around the throne, saints were worshiping God. I could see it happening as we spoke.

As we spoke about the glory, Sister Ruth said that it was running through her spirit. She said that it was like the train of His glory. It's moving all of the time. When Sister Ruth talked about dancing in the streets of Jerusalem, she was referring to the glory as a Jerusalem experience. God said that Jerusalem would be "a praise" in all the Earth. He wants us to release what He is doing in His headquarters. You don't teach it. You catch it.

I didn't know that Sister Ruth was going to talk about the fire. I just saw a wall of fire as she relayed the story about the pastor and the Mennonite woman. I didn't know that she was going to say that there was fire dripping off of the pastor. I just saw the fire as Sister Ruth told the story. I said, "Oh, God. I'm on fire!" I was reliving it. It began just before she told us what was going to happen.

There was a wall of fire coming into the room as Sister Ruth and I were talking. I saw the wall of fire coming toward us, not once but twice. It was brushing. This is what the Lord wants us to have. It is repeated twice in the Bible. I just believe that it is going out. It is going forth to everyone. Just receive it right now.

I want to tell you that I was experiencing fire like I have previously only experienced in Heaven. It's amazing when you get a couple of people together and you start to feel it in this realm. It's a supernatural act. In Heaven, we don't have the limitations that we have down here. You can experience all kinds of things in Heaven. There are no limitations up there.

But when you experience it in the flesh, it is a supernatural act that is ordained from the throne of God. What we experienced in the interview was hard for me to imagine as something to experience so strongly in the flesh. That's because I first felt it when I walked on the sapphire stone of Heaven. That fire was so hot that I almost couldn't make it across the floor in Heaven. But the Lord told me during our interview that what Sister Ruth and I were feeling is something that is permanent.

Sister Ruth said that she saw something on the floor that looked like it was laid out, like a stone. It might have been a coal or something from the altar. She said that she saw what looked like a big blue stone, or maybe a coal, laid out at my feet. God wants to manifest His ways and His workings.

During our interview, I was really cooking! I just believe that this was (and is) being imparted. This rarely happens to this extent. I'm not kidding you. But the anointing is outside of time, because God isn't constrained by our realm. The anointing is given by the Holy Spirit. It remains upon us and our words, whether spoken or written.

Everyone, just raise your hands. Point your hands toward your phone, device, or your book. Just receive the fire of this new move of God. It's the glory of God. There is a fire in the glory and it is just one of those things that is happening right now. That "right now" is today. Just take it right now. Receive it. This is ordained by God for you. The power of the fire of the Holy Spirit is cleansing you right now. Just receive it by faith. Praise God.

Next, we'll hear from Sister Ruth about the fire and then we will ask you to receive her prayer of impartation.

(*Sister Ruth is now speaking.*) Beloved saints, even if it is uncomfortable, we need to let the fire of the Holy Spirit consume us. True worship releases the glory and the fire. Let it ignite you. Jump into the fire. The fire is cleansing. It causes your flesh to cooperate with God.

The fire comes so that we can touch the nations. The Lord says, "I own you. I bought you. Now I am going to ignite you for this generation." He is igniting you because you need to move to the next step. He wants us to catch on fire and begin to move with Him.

The Lord wants you to go beyond the places you have been. Go beyond the control that has been upon your life. Just get rid of the old. Get rid of that religious thing that has held you back for so long. Use the tools that God has given you. Begin with your faith. God has given everyone a measure of faith. Your family won't necessarily understand. Remember how the people said, "Is this Jesus, Joseph's son?" They didn't understand.

Let the Holy Spirit work out what you don't know. Let Him work it out. There's a lot He wants to work out. God is a creative force. Let Him cleanse your heart and your mouth. Let Him do it. It's important to let God cleanse you from all of the old ways. Cry a lot. Let a cleansing stream come from Heaven. Let the river flow.

I'm going to pray a prayer of impartation over you. You may or may not feel something happen, but just open your heart and receive it by faith.

> *Thank You, Lord. Lord, we send Your fire after the people. Let it consume them. God, let that desire consume them so that they want to know You, Lord, in a way they haven't before. God, even like in the Bible with the Hebrew children, Lord, when they got in the fire, You were there with them (Daniel 3:25). It's not that kind of fire. It's a greater kind.*
>
> *Lord, there's a greater anointing. There's a greater making. There's a greater understanding. As You said, "I'm a consuming fire." We want to be consumed by Your desires—consumed, Lord, in Your delight, and in what You want to do in the Earth. God, show us this so that we can step out of the old and into the new to the goodness of the Lord. Where You're creating, Lord, new hearts, You're creating, Lord, new desires. Lord, You're creating more than they have had before. Let them catch hold of it, Lord.*
>
> *Let them be ignited. God, let the wind of the Spirit get into that fire. Everywhere they go, Lord, may there be more fires built in more neighborhoods—in cities and*

stores and shopping centers. I believe You, Lord. They will go and they will carry. You're carrying them in Your chariot for the glory of the Lord to be revealed. God, we thank You for it, for the revelation of Jesus Christ, Lord, and Him only. We thank You for it. In Your name we pray. Amen.

Saints, right now, put your hands up and begin to praise the Lord and sing. I'm going to give you the rest of your song here as a prophetic word.

(Sister Ruth sings the following words.) You've got a wind in your mouth. You've got the winds gathered from the winds of the Spirit to gather and worship. Let your voice bring forth the path of the Lord. It's a river inside of you. Bring it forth. Oh, He's expressing. Let your voice revive what God wants to do. Let your voice revive what He wants to do.

Let Him bring forth. Bring forth. Bring forth. Bring forth what the Lord is doing in you. Break forth. Break forth what He's working in the Earth. Let it be seen. Let it shine. Oh, He said that He is looking for a prophetic voice, the voice of the dove, the voice of the Spirit, to bring forth what He wants to do.

Let your voice put in motion, put in motion, not slow motion. We're talking about locomotion. We're talking about the train of the Lord, the glory of the Lord, the glory of what God is doing in you.

Let the sound of all of Heaven ring like a bell, like an alarm. Let it ring like an alarm of what God is doing. It's a voice, a voice. Let it be put in motion. Come on. You'll save yourself a lot of unworthy time. You'll save yourself and you will be using what God has given you.

(*Sister Ruth stops singing and continues speaking.*) Remember that your voice is your weapon. God wants us to speak from the heavens. The way God speaks isn't like the way we speak in the natural world. Our mind can't even enter into the Spirit. God speaks into our spirit. He gives us His plan for our life.

He has given us eternity to work in the Earth. You were born to live forever. The Lord is our forever. You were born to know Him and to know His ways. He said that His ways are past finding out. So sing and praise the Lord with your voice. Let the glory ring forth and bring forth the will of the Lord.

GLORY ENLARGES

Sister Ruth here, saints. Some of us have read Isaiah 54:1 many times. It says, "Sing, O barren." Have you ever felt like you were barren? You know, you try to worship, you try to touch the glory, but it just isn't there. You know there is something else. You are reaching out for it with everything, and I literally mean with everything. You feel the strain at the same time you are trying to make room for it to come in.

God is enlarging you to receive the covenant, plan, and strategies of what He is doing in the heavens. He says, "Sing, O barren, you who have not borne! Break forth. Here it is" (Isaiah 54:1).

Break into singing and cry aloud! The cry will come with the enlargement. It breaks it open to receive more. He is showing us how to do it. It's so easy.

You don't have to go somewhere. You don't have to spend money, but it would be nice if we gave more. Give yourself to the Lord. Give everything that is within you. Give Him your heart. This is what He is talking about.

God will reveal, in all you do, what is shaping, turning, and moving in the Earth. He tells us in Isaiah 54:2, "Enlarge the place of your tent." This talks about our place of tabernacling with God. He wants to tabernacle with us. Enlarge the place of your tabernacle. Enlarge the place of your tent.

He said, "Enlarge." He is talking about all who want to be true worshipers. Allow Him to stretch it out as far as the eye of the Spirit can see. Stretch out. Stretch your cords. Don't stay in the same place. Don't have the same song. See what God is doing and declare the works of the Lord.

Stretch out the curtains of your dwelling. Don't spare. Don't limit God. Don't limit what He can do. Know that He is God. He is worthy of all the joy, shouting, dancing, and sacrifice.

God wants to give us revelation upon revelation. He wants to give us true worship. He wants us to see the God of our heart and our spirit, the God of our making. He wants us to see other aspects of His greatness and His knowledge without end. We will see it forever.

Knowledge is one of the gifts of the Spirit. It will be the only gift we will have in Heaven that we had on Earth. Once we go to

Heaven, we won't need the other gifts that are for our use while we are on the Earth.

When God enlarges you, people will come from far and wide. You will never fear if you don't have income or other means. He will cause things to multiply thirty, sixty, and a hundredfold. He will overwhelm you with the joy of your song through your relationship with Him. You will be singing all day long, "Look what the Lord hath done!"

This is the time of *seeing and hearing*. You will always give away the "less." Never fear that you have given away something precious. He has something far more precious, more overwhelming, and more worth looking at.

He said, "I am going to give you eyes to see." The Bible says that we "see not" (Jeremiah 5:21). Two of our senses are smelling and tasting. Smelling is direction. The nose is direct. Tasting is enjoying and working the magnificence of the Lord.

We want to be people who want enlargement. God says, "Come on. Stretch yourself out there. Make room for Me. Make room. I've got something else. I'm going to move into your house, into your kingdom."

You will know when it's time to go here or there. You will feel it birthing inside of you. You will actually feel like you are pregnant. I'm serious! In dreams, I was walking around with my maternity dress on. I would say, "Look at me." Suddenly, I had this great enlargement. God wants to bring enlargement. When it comes, you expand.

It's a kind of painless childbirth. It's painless when you are birthing in the Spirit and when you move in the glory realm.

There is room in the glory. There is expansion. There is enlargement. You need that no man teach you. You just know. It's birthed. The baby is here. It's alive. It's walking. Hallelujah. It is talking before it is walking.

You want to be like Evangelist Sister Aimee Semple McPherson.[1] The end of her ministry wasn't really what we thought it should be, but the woman had vision. She saw enlargement before it came. Hollywood came over to help her. We don't hear about Hollywood coming over to help us. We need to pray for some of that blessing of enlargement to come our way.

To some people, it's not a blessing. It's almost a curse. That's because they don't know how to use it. But God wants to save them. He wants everyone to sow into the future so that enlargement can come.

He is saying to us, strengthen. Strengthen! Let your roots go deep. Strengthen your stakes. Pour some oil on it with some fasting and prayer. Give a little more. *Open up to the wisdom of God.* Do what doesn't feel good and what is uncomfortable. Go outside your comfort zone.

Wherever you go, don't look for a reason not to eat their food or sleep on their bed. Look for a reason to get there. People need God to come and visit. They need someone who has been to Heaven to come and see them and to bring them the light.

I have ministered and entertained a lot because my portion in ministry was always to take care of others. I was to take care of the minister first. I prepared the bed for every speaker who came to our ministry camp for twenty-some years. I prepared the room. I gave the man or woman of God a glass of water. Take care of others first and God will take care of you. Shelter in Him. He will protect you.

One day, I was getting ready to go for therapy. Suddenly I thought, *You need to pray for the house.* So I sat down and said, "Lord, I know this is a short prayer, but I really need Your help. Cover my house. Cover everything around it." I forgot to say, "Cover the walls and trees."

That day, a car ran into my yard, but it missed the house. It didn't touch it even though it came right up to the wall and tore things down. Suppose I hadn't prayed that prayer!

As Brother Kevin says, God wants you to know that He is busy taking care of your affairs. When you have given your heart to Him, He is watching over everything concerning your heart. He overshadows you daily and brings you under His umbrella of protection.

I really love where the Word says, "And your descendants." He is talking about your descendants. Those are your children, your mother, father, and whoever else is in your household. He said, "They will inherit the nations" (Psalm 82:8).

Because you have been faithful to God, He will be faithful to you. You will expand to the right and to the left. You will move from the place that you have been to the place that God wants you to go.

We have an awesome God. He's an awesome God! Call Him awesome. How do you explain awesome? It's beyond words. No one really deserves that word. People use the word *awesome* too casually. That word only belongs to the Lord Jesus Christ, the God of man and of all the Earth.

We can say "God." We should hesitate to say the name that is above every name because of the power in the name! It does something when we just mention His name. His name *enlarges*. Did you know that?

I was a Christian before I was saved. We had a doctrine that was a little different than what the Lord says. My parents thought that I went a little wild. I did. I wanted it all or I didn't want any of it.

Now I have three granddaughters. Before the third one was born, the Lord spoke about the coming child. At the time, I didn't know that my daughter-in-law was with child and neither did she.

One day, she was asking the Lord what she should give me for my birthday. The Lord surprised us all. He said, "Tell her she is going to be a grandmother." That's how my daughter-in-law found out that she was pregnant. So she came to tell me.

I was given exactly six months to hold that grandchild. You see, I have had very few Christmases because of missionary work. I'm not complaining. I knew I would miss family and things. But the Lord told me suddenly, "You will not live to see these grandchildren grow up."

I thought He meant that I was going to go home young or that He was going to take them. You have to read into what God shares with you. What He meant was that I was going to be busy in one field and He was going to use them in another.

Their mother, Margaret, was a missionary to Ecuador before she married my son. Of course, the children are a leaf from that same tree. Two of the children were about eighteen months apart.

Margaret called me to ask me a question when her children were around six or seven years of age. She asked, "What do you think about leaving your granddaughters in Ecuador?"

I suddenly became very quiet. Then I asked, "Leave?" She replied, "Yes. Let's leave them with a sitter for a little while." I didn't debate with her. As their mother, she had first priority. I knew that she was spiritual, so I asked, "What is God telling you?"

She answered, "I think it would be a good plan." The Lord had said to her, "What they need to know, they will learn in a hurry." She knew the people of Ecuador well. She had been there for a few years, and she knew the language.

At one time she had fasted for forty days, drinking only water. Halfway through her fast, God gave her the ability to know and speak the entire Spanish language. She was able to go all over South America.

What a beautiful person. When you looked at her, you wanted to laugh because she laughed all of the time. Her laughter sounded like someone playing a piano. God was playing her heart. He wants to play your heart, too. I finally said, "Okay, I won't stop you or limit you. I'm trusting God."

I would make sure that I had all of eternity to talk with those children and that God would do a replay of what happened in their younger years. He will make up for what you didn't get. Do you realize what I am saying?

Those granddaughters were put through the highest schools in the land. One went to a top university. Another one studied to be a nurse but ended up being a social worker. Now she is studying to be a pastor somewhere. I'll just declare that.

I realize that I don't know enough about God. When Margaret and I had that discussion, I understood what God had meant when He told me, "You will not see them grow up, but they will inherit the nations." Those little girls have skipped all over the world. They have been throughout South America and Africa. God will enlarge your family and their reach. Let God give you the nations. He says, "Ask of Me and I'll give you the nations for an inheritance."

I want you to put your hands up. In the morning and many times at night, I put my hands into the air and reach for God. I surrender all. I tell Him, "I want more. Lord, I need more." Our hands are our defense. When they are raised, it means, "I surrender all, Lord." Go ahead and ask Him. Say, "Lord, You said to ask of You and You would give to me. It's a small thing I am asking." Ask Him for your inheritance. Ask Him for the nations.

When we come into that place of knowing Him, we know that He is all we have ever searched for. He is all we ever need. Your life will become divinely ordered. You will take steps in the right direction. You'll never lack. You won't have to be concerned about what you need because God knows your need before you even ask.

Just move in the pleasantries, in the joys, and in the goodness of the Lord. Watch your soul rejoice because of the enlargement. You will be asking, "How can my soul bear all the blessings, but for the enlargement of the Lord?"

GLORY WORKS

It's Kevin, friends. Like Sister Ruth, I have seen a lot of miracles and healings in my life. God says that we should ask and it shall be given (Matthew 7:7). It's by faith. We are to desire miracles. Jesus did miracles everywhere. He did good. He did miracles more than anything. He waited for people to cry out. He wants us to ask Him for more. We are to ask the one who has it all and who knows how to provide.

Understand that we can't be "good enough" to receive a miracle. It's something that we ask for simply because we are in need. Ask God for a miracle. We ask for this gift to meet a need. Jesus was sent as an ambassador to advance His Father's Kingdom. One of the ways this would occur was through miracles. Jesus would heal people who yelled out, "Thou son of David, have mercy on me!"

Many people wonder what this "David" thing is all about. When people said "Son of David," they were saying that Jesus was the Messiah. People recognized Him as their Savior. The reward for that recognition was healing and deliverance.

The gifts and callings of the Lord are without repentance. He gives them to us because He loves us. God doesn't take gifts away even if we do things that aren't pleasing to Him. The gifts He gives will still operate. He will still work when people are away from Him. God's miracles are a free gift. He uses them in the body of Christ to raise it up, to change it, and to heal and enlarge it. He works miracles in the church to make people who and what He wants them to be.

God will always help you. It's like a local call, not a long distance one. God is inside of you. Understand that He won't give you a barrel full of money if you haven't handled money properly in the past, but He will work miracles to help you get out of debt. He is the miracle worker. Fine-tune yourself to learn of Him, and miracles will happen.

God works in your life even when you are still away from Him. Our gifts work as long as we don't curse God or His Holy Spirit. He isn't going to operate in that. He won't be spoiled by that.

He says, "Freely you receive. Freely give" (Matthew 10:8). I love that. We can be kind even when we don't want to be, and God will honor our kindness. Whatever you do in His name is favored by Him. People who don't even know God can be kind. God blesses them because kindness is a treasure that is precious unto Him. It's a gift of the Spirit (Galatians 5:22-23).

We want to use the gifts that God gives us and we want to be in our right mind and spirit when we use them. We want to live righteously when we use our gifts, lest a worse thing come upon us (John 5:14). Let's return to Sister Ruth's story now, as she reveals more to us about how the glory has worked in her life. You will see that there are some things that the enemy will try to use to take us out. But when we operate in the gifts, God preserves us.

(*Sister Ruth is now speaking.*) When I was young, my family never visited a doctor. My father would pray for his family and we would be healed. For example, my mother had heart disease. When she was dying, she said, "Lord, will You let me live to raise my children?" He healed her! You see, many times we simply need to ask God the right questions. She gave the Lord a reason why it was important that she live.

Brother Kevin tells us that it's important to ask the right questions. You want to be used by God. My mother had five children at the time that the Lord healed her. She literally jumped up out of the bed and danced all around! She got an instant healing. It was the glory working in the prayers.

We usually get bad news when there are snowstorms or rainstorms. God wants you to know what is happening in the *good news*. He wants us to see in the supernatural. So let the Spirit of revelation take you higher and deeper into the glory realm.

When you go to a ballgame, there is a space they want you to occupy for the game. However, the ball can go out of the park. God has given you all of the room that you will ever need. The glory brings a life in the Lord that isn't limited by the natural world. Make room for the glory and allow it to work in you and through you.

Dr. Renny McLean, a prophetic minister, wrote a book called *Eternity Invading Time*. It has dimension from beginning to end. One year, Renny came to our ministry camp. He was talking about the great miracles that he had seen and that God had proven through him.

God had told Renny not to go to Bible school. He told him, "I'm going to teach you." God chooses certain people to use. Do you know that sometimes we aren't His first or even His second choice? He isn't looking for perfection in our flesh. He is going to perfect us by His Spirit.

At our meeting, Renny was telling us about a man who was born without eyes. I'm going to paraphrase. The Lord said, "I'm going to put the eyeballs in your hands." Renny went over and put his hands on the man's face. Suddenly, the man was able to see!

I was thinking, *What would God give me?* I didn't think He would bring me somebody's leg or arm. I know that sounds kind of foolish. While I was thinking about what God would give me, I suddenly felt something in my hand. It felt as if I was holding a man's eardrum. I just knew it was in my hand. Renny was getting people to come up with their miracle in their hand, so I jumped up.

I knew I had it. Then it disappeared. I tried to find it. I couldn't see it, but I knew it was there in the Spirit. A woman was standing next to me, so I asked, "Would anybody know anything about an ear, nose, and eye surgeon?" The woman said, "My son is one!" So, I said, "Do you know what an eardrum looks like?" And she answered, "Yes!"

God had it all prepared. Remember that He said, "I will prepare a table before you" (Psalm 23:5). The miracles are there all the time. I knew that someone in front of me was born without an ear drum.

A man was standing right in front of me, so I asked him, "Sir, do you have a hearing problem?" He said, "I was born without an eardrum." I replied, "Well, I've got it in my hand!" I reached over and put my hand on top of his ear. Then he said, "I hear! I hear! I hear!" Praise God! I have been waiting for more of those miracles!

It's so nice to know that people are going to be made complete. God is going to use you to help people become complete. That's a miracle! I've had this happen again and again. God would create things for me during church services. One day I needed something. I desperately needed it. I was standing there in the front, but I didn't want to disturb the people. I'm not going to tell you what it was that I needed. The camera was looking my way. I was trying to hide myself.

When the people stepped back, there on the floor was the exact thing that I needed. I don't know where it came from. God rescued me! He will do it in a second. He wants to do it! He wants us to eat that heavenly manna from His table all of the time. God loves you and wants you to be without want, without lack, and without your natural desires. Peace, love, and fulfillment come in the ease of the glory.

People know about a natural kind of love. Read the *Song of Solomon.* I used to think that somebody put the wrong book in the Bible. That's because I had never encountered such love. The Lord calls us His "darling." For a long time, I couldn't even say that word. That's a precious word to carry into your heart. I'm sure you can understand that.

We want to hear those conversations, those *love notes.* God wrote His love letter to us in the Bible. In the *Songs,* it says, "My beloved comes with rings of beryl" (Songs 5:14). I didn't really know what that color looked like. Another Scripture verse says, "Who can find a virtuous woman?" (Proverb 31:10 KJV). I was thinking of natural things. It says, "For her price is far above rubies." Think about that for a moment.

I got so excited about that Scripture. I even went through a snowstorm to preach a sermon on how "my beloved comes." I asked the Lord, "Lord, am I Your beloved? If I am, where is my ring of beryl?" That's what I said. I didn't really expect anything.

That night, a lady showed up at our meeting while I was talking about my beloved. The Lord had said to the woman, "I want you to give her your mother's beryl ring." This woman drove through a snowstorm for eighty miles to deliver that ring to me. She went eighty miles in a snowstorm! She said, "God awakened me and said to give you this ring."

The ring story goes on and on. One day, I saw another woman's face in the ring, so I gave the ring to her. I found out that she had sold some of her rings to purchase two tickets to travel to the Philippines.

The woman's father wasn't a believer. He had cancer and he was dying. His family wanted to see him before he departed. When he saw the woman's new beryl ring, he thought it was really crazy to have sold her other rings just to buy two plane tickets to see him, but consider this. The beryl ring's appraisal value ended up equaling the price of the woman's plane tickets.

Listen saints. It's a big thing when God does this. It may not seem important, but look what God did. He created many things for that woman to have that ring. And when she told her father about where she got the beryl ring, he got saved and then God took him to Heaven. Praise God!

A while later, I again asked God about the rubies. I said, "If I'm a virtuous woman..." You know how women are. We see the luster. The Lord began working on that question when I asked it. He starts working the moment you ask Him. We may think when delay comes that foolishness or troubles are going on, but that isn't what is happening. God is giving you the *cost* of what you have asked of Him.

Look at everything the Lord has done for Brother Kevin and Sister Kathi. They went through major changes just to get where they are, yet the journey has been wonderful for them. Sometimes, the benefits of the Lord can make you feel like a child on Christmas day. It's been wonderful. The journey is wonderful.

One year, a young man showed up at our ministry camp. I knew that he didn't have family as the holidays were upon us, so I invited him to stay with us through Thanksgiving. After that holiday ended, the young man wanted to leave. He felt like it wasn't his territory. I said, "Oh, we're all family, just stay." He was a little shy, so everywhere Mary went, that lamb went with me. He got in my car. Everywhere I went, he was "pedaling" right behind me.

When Christmas came, he felt that he didn't have anything to give us. No one here does. We are all living by faith. Whatever God does is okay. We are just enjoying the moments. We had an open house for those who didn't have a home. We invited people over for Christmas dinner. We had guests for twenty-some years on such eventful days.

The young man said to me, "I really don't have anything." Then I saw him quietly exit the room. Later, he returned with a tissue in his hand. He said to me, "I have a little something to give." He placed the balled-up tissue in my hand.

I couldn't imagine what was inside. I wasn't thinking about anything great. I opened the tissue to find two hundred rubies! We had one hundred and fifty guests at the breakfast table. God was saying, "You are all virtuous to Me." I realized the Scripture verse in that moment and thought, *I'm not going to be selfish here. This is not a moment for that.*

I never got one of those diamonds, or rubies. Well, now that I have said it, I might be able to get diamonds! I left the little tissue in the closet. I never retrieved it. Many years went by. I recently said, "Lord, You know, I never got one of those rubies." I said it, but first God brought it to my mind, even though I don't wear a lot of jewelry.

One of my friends was at an estate sale. There was a big ruby, sapphire, and (I think) opal ring. There were twelve jewels in all. Twelve is a lot of jewels. But in the Scripture, there are twelve stones on the priest's breastplate. That ring had leaves on it like I had never seen. They were all gold. There was more than one ruby on the ring. They were just like the ones I had left behind.

Do you see how God will multiply your obedience? He will multiply what you give Him. God is in the business of multiplying. In fact, everything you put your hands to will multiply. You will be saying, "Lord, how can I take care of all of this?" Well, just go and get some more help! Gather others to help you.

Do you know that God will go after those who are still on the outside? We have to know all of the moves that the Lord has made to get us to the place where we are. What God has done is precious. For a long time, I didn't feel the loveliness of that. But one day, I looked in the mirror and God began to show me how He sees His beloved bride.

The Lord said to me, "Oh, will you marry Me?" In other words, He was saying, "Will you trust Me to take care of you? I want to be your husband. I want to be your husband and I will take care of you. Trust Me and listen." He was telling me that He wasn't going to give me everything I wanted at one time. But as I prospered in my soul, He began to add to me.

I always had a spiffy little sports car, but for years I didn't have a car. God had my car. I had given my car and everything else away. One day, God bought me an old car. Everyone made fun of it, but it got me to the store and to church. I eventually gave the car away.

One person had made fun of my old car, so God spoke to them. That person got a brand-new Lincoln. Before they went on a trip, the Lord said to them, "I want you to let her drive your car while you are away." The person returned with a new Cadillac. I ended up being able to keep the Lincoln, all because the people had made fun of my old car.

We have to be careful with what we say and how we think. When you move and walk in the glory, you have to order your words and how you feel about things. You have to be careful how you evaluate things and take care with what you say. Be careful how you lay words upon others. What we say should please God's heart. We are to lift Him up in all that we do and say. We will learn by experience.

The glory realm isn't like an anointing. It's a totally new and higher realm. You are representing the Lord when you walk in the glory realm. People around you know it. They know there is a higher way that you are walking in. They recognize it and want it. They want the glory and the blessings that come from walking in it.

We have to be transformed. The glory brings transformation. God told me, "Let Me show you what the bride looks like." I want to look all gold and transparent, don't you? Jesus can see right through you. When you fall in love with Him, you don't see any image of anything else. You see only the beauty of who He is and who you are in Him.

We are His beloved bride. In the *Song of Solomon,* it says, "I'm lovesick." That means more than what we have read or even know. Jesus wants us to go after Him with great passion. He wants to heal everything in our body, our spirit, and our life. He loves us so much! He is the greatest provider. We find all that we need when we meet Him in the glory realm.

You know, there are mansions in Heaven that we will see one day. I'm planning to live in the New Jerusalem. God doesn't want us to be consumed with limitations, with rings, cars, or any other material things. He wants us to be free. This freedom and this Kingdom that He offers us is eternal. Indeed, it is the most priceless treasure we can ever hope to receive.

NOTE

1. Aimee Semple McPherson was a Canadian Pentecostal evangelist who, in the 1920s and 1930s, pioneered the use of broadcast media in religious services. She also founded the Foursquare Church, an early megachurch.

Four

GLORY LIFE

Lord, we bless You in the name of Jesus. Lord, I pray that we will move according to Your plan. I decree that prophets, evangelists, and seers are going to come forth from many nations for the salvation of the nations. You are going to have an army of people who know You and who will not break ranks. God, You will have a representative. We thank You that they will know it and prepare. They will put aside the old, for the new to come forth. Thank You, Lord, for the vision. Amen.

—Sister Ruth Carneal

KNOW THE SEASONS

Friends, it's Sister Ruth again. Do you know that you are the pleasure of the Lord? He takes pleasure in manifesting who He is through us. We are entering a time when it seems as if we are going to be entertaining the Lord. He is taking His pleasure in us.

We are coming into a time of seeing like we have never seen before. God is adjusting the distance. He is adjusting in our hearts how we perceive the heavens, so we will know the times.

We won't see church in the same ways that we have in the past. We won't be using our gifts in the same ways we have been. We will know when God is pouring out. We are entering a new day, a new season, and a new life.

This is the day when God is moving. There is a wonderful new way of thinking. We aren't going to be drinking the old wine. We will drink the new wine. We will partake of things the Lord has prepared for us. It feels to me as if He is presenting His glory with great joy.

There are a lot of teachings on the seasons and timings of God. A lot of times we don't understand God's timing. It isn't like our calendar. You will just know the seasons because they will be set in your heart like a clock.

Every time God changes a season, He places a greater anointing, a greater weight of glory upon your life. He puts a new mantle on you so you can do the unusual. You will go higher.

The body is undergoing beauty treatments, just as Esther did. She endured six months of perfumes and oils. Then she had six months of other things.

There are seasons in life when things sound quiet. There are dry seasons when nothing is happening. Even so, God never sleeps. He is working to make you His own. You want to get this into your heart. Be possessed by the goodness of the Lord.

There is a strong stirring in the Spirit. We are being stirred up. We have emotions that God wants to explain. We are seeing Him in another light. It's the day of brightness, the day of the coming of the Lord.

He is coming to make these adjustments and to put knowledge in us of what He is doing. There is a new freedom and a new declaration. There is a level of victory we have never experienced before. It's wonderful! God is giving us the better things.

There are Scriptures that talk about the last days. God asks us, "Are we His people?" Does He know you? Do you have a relationship with Jesus Christ? God said, "I am going to take My people where no big ship or little boat with oars has ever been" (Isaiah 33:21). That's what it says. You haven't been to this place. We haven't been this way before.

God requires change every time He takes us into something new. Just as there are seasons in the natural world, there are seasons in the Lord that we are to move through. With every new season, more is required. We are maturing in the Lord.

God wants us to learn how to put Him first. He is continually weighing things. He is developing us and moving us to exercise our gifts. We are growing, learning, and transforming. Physical and spiritual growth takes place over time.

When I was ten or twelve years old, I remember coming home one day and telling my mother, "Mother, I have met some people today and they are different. They look like Christians, but they're not. I can't explain it to you, Mother. The people had these curls and black clothes and these little stockings."

I told her that they were somehow connected to God. My mother didn't know what I saw. I don't think she ever saw a Jewish person in cultural dress, but I was fascinated. I was quite young at the time. I didn't understand the dress code of the Orthodox Jewish people. Later on, I learned they are God's chosen people. They belong to Him.

Sometimes God will set you up in a situation. It may feel as if He is trying to embarrass you, but He isn't. What He is doing is shaking you up. He is trying to shake things loose to separate the earthly realm from your spirit.

It seems a little funny now, but God uses our situations to show us things. Before I began to travel, the Lord dressed me like a little rabbi. He had one person give me a brand-new black coat. Another person gave me a big, wide-brimmed black hat. I was also given a black and white scarf, black gloves, a black purse, black boots, and a black suitcase. I wouldn't figure out what was happening until I got to Europe.

The Lord told me, "Your heart belongs to Judah." I thought to myself, *I don't know any Judah, Lord*. I didn't have a boyfriend or a husband at the time. Eventually, I realized that I was identifying with the Jewish people.

As I studied the Word, God opened my understanding. He has called me to be a worshiper. I am called to worship Him and to allow the river to flow inside of me. That river is connected to the throne of God.

In a later season of my life, I heard a rabbi speak named Jack Zimmerman. At the time he worked with Jonathan Burns of *Jewish Voice*. Brother Jack came to preach about the biblical festivals and traditions surrounding Passover and Pentecost.

He was standing on a beautiful carpet, which was holy ground. When he finished speaking, I saw two angels come in. They picked up the carpet, shook it out, rolled it up, and carried it back to its resting place. That day Brother Jack got a new promotion in the Lord. He moved to higher ground.

He had shared about the feasts of the Bible and how in the millennium we will once again practice the feasts. God desires that we have a feast every day. He wants us to be seated at the table of the Lord in the joys and delights of all that He desires for us.

GOD HAS TIMES AND SEASONS

Many times we want to pray ourselves out of something, like a position that God has put us into. He is trying to teach us His ways, His paths, His directions, and His loving kindness. With God, it's new every morning.

God does things that many people can miss. That's why we "Pentecostals," and those who really know God, are laughing all of the time. People think we heard a joke. No, it's the delight of the Lord and recognizing how He is moving. He is expressing what He is doing through all that we do for Him.

God may allow certain things to occur in order to tear us away from what we know. He will change the order of things. He wants to change the order of our church services. He does this to bring us onto higher ground where He is.

The best thing to do in this season is not to have a plan. Just enter in. Step into the Holy of Holies with the Lord. Take off whatever the day has put upon you, and put on His robes of righteousness. Get into His presence and love on Him with your voice.

As you grow in the seasons of the Lord, your voice will begin to change. It will have a different sound to it. I'm not talking about the way our voice changes as we mature. I am saying that your voice will begin to carry the sound of His presence and His love.

Brother Kevin is very astute. He tells us that we need to learn how to be aware of the seasons and timing of God. They differ from those of our worldly calendars, although God created calendars and clocks for us. We instinctively know when to wake up and when to go to bed. God puts these cycles into us so we will learn how to come into the calendar and time charts of Heaven.

I know that we sometimes wonder, "Is God ever going to do something?" You may feel this expectancy, like a mother does when she is about to bring forth a child. She almost knows the day and the hour. We will know the times and the seasons.

There are seasons of waiting upon the Lord. You can't pray in your natural language for very long, because you will run out of things to say. That's why it's good to get into that river of praying in the Spirit. It carries you from glory to glory and from secret to secret.

You may be in a season when you are being tested or your character is being formed. There will come a time when you are promoted because you have passed your test. There are even times when you feel as if God may have forgotten about you, but He never forgets!

(*Kevin is now speaking.*) Friends, it takes total surrender to follow the Lord. Many times He heals through fasting and total surrender to Him. He said, "Your ways are not My ways" (Isaiah 55:8). Prayer, fasting, and waiting upon the Lord are the easiest ways to enter into the next season. That's the threefold cord mentioned earlier. We are to seek the face of the Lord for this new depth, this new way that He is working.

All the money and teachers in the world can't teach you how the glory operates. The secrets of God's heart are known by revelation and by searching His heart. It is important to desire revelation. You will be declaring revelations that you have never heard before. Each one will strengthen your walk with the Lord.

There is a place where you know what God wants. You will step into it. It's a place of great possibilities and prosperity. You are not teaching it or telling people how to get it. It just happens because you are moving in the "nows" of God.

There is always a now. The Bible says, "Now faith is" (Hebrews 11:1). It's now. It is happening right now. It's not tomorrow or next week. It's right now. We are walking in the future and what God wants in our life. Be hungry for that.

We are to prepare the way of the Lord. Prepare it. That means to get ready for whatever is coming. You are ready and waiting for it. There are no surprises or limitations. There will suddenly be an ability to move in the Lord with the heavens. Go with it.

God gives us the seasons and timings. There may never be another opportunity to move closer to the Lord, like we have today. Your life is going to be a sacrifice. You will become a living sacrifice. He said, "Present yourself as a living sacrifice, holy and acceptable unto the Lord" (Romans 12:1).

RECOGNIZE ANGELS

(*Kevin continues his thoughts.*) As believers, we are heirs of the Kingdom. God uses His ministering angels to get our attention and to minister to us. He says, "Aren't they all ministering spirits sent forth to minister to the heirs of salvation?" (Hebrews 1:14).

Angels bring revelations of Heaven. They bring from the throne what is necessary for today. We will become more aware of their presence because they move in the glory realm. They will manifest more and more as we step into our calling. Angels are more involved in our lives than people realize.

Sister Ruth Carneal has told me that there is an angel for every church. She says that you have to surround yourself with angels and she is right. God is doing something different in every church and that's good news. The Word says, "Let the church hear what the Spirit is speaking unto them" (Revelation 2:29). The church has to change its thinking. If we come into the wrong thoughts, we grieve the Holy Spirit.

Did you know that when you worship, angels come to hear you? That's because you are identifying with what God is doing. They come to hear from you what they hear in the heavens. They do what God orders them to do, but all they can say is, "Holy, Holy, Holy." They keep saying it because every time they say "Holy," they see another measure of Holy. God says, "Worship the Lord in the Spirit of holiness" (Romans 1:4). Our holy God is looking for people who are holy and living in truth. Let's listen in now for more of Sister Ruth's story.

(*Sister Ruth continues sharing.*) Beloved, our spirit is always crying out for more. The Holy Spirit wants to take us into more. I had a hunger to move into a higher realm. I felt there was something more and I needed to know. I would question God about realms of the Spirit. He made me hunger for more. I was always reaching for it.

I finally met up with a group of people who were moving in this realm. For years, God had been leading them by the glory. I had never heard of the kind of visions that He brought them. I didn't understand the work of the glory. I didn't know it was bringing Heaven into the Earth.

I have had many encounters with angels. I have become very aware of them next to me. Many of them have been in my house! Listen, when you come into another realm, you may feel like you are still in the natural. But you are actually in another realm where you are seeing the movements of angels with your eyes.

Folks, holy angels are God's messengers. I have seen angels come into church services when we are truly in the place of Zion. We are worshiping from the mountain. I have seen some strange things moving through the air. I have thought, *What is this? What are these things going through the air?* They looked like jewelry settings that hold stones. I have seen God putting depth and height into people. I have seen jewels being put upon people's breastplates.

It's time to come into the glory realm, the garden of the Lord. It's the realm of the heavenlies, a realm where angels sing. There is a lovely song by Joshua Mills called "The Glory Realm." The song came from Heaven one day as we were on the way to speak during the Feast of Tabernacles.

Sister Ruth Heflin usually had a song for every movement she operated in. She would always fast for at least forty days for every nation she went to—forty days! She went to all the nations in the world. They are stamped in her book *Harvest Glory*. If you read it, you will feel like you are there, moving in the pages with her. You will feel caught away.

The glory catches you up into another hemisphere. You enter another place. You must be willing to really die for it. Just let go and let God. In the glory, we learn how to move. I learned timing in God. I learned not to get ahead of God but to follow Him. Timing is very important.

I have found that the angels will manifest when and where God is working. You will feel and see them around you as they protect you, deliver messages, or minister to you in other ways. They are the escorts, warriors, and conductors of the glory realm of Heaven. Brother Kevin can certainly tell you some stories about his own angel visitations. They are quite profound.

(*Kevin now shares his thoughts.*) I would like to bless you, friends, with a brief story. One time I needed to talk to the Lord. I prayed that God would visit and that I would have an angel visitation. I had never asked for that before, but I thought that it would be nice if the Lord would visit. Later that night, I awoke to the feeling that someone's physical foot had kicked me in the side.

I looked around, but no one was there. I fell back asleep but soon got kicked again. I awoke and fell back to sleep again. The next morning, I realized that the Lord had sent an angel to awaken me and to speak to me, just as I had requested.

It would be several years before I would get the answer to the question I had been seeking the night that angel came. I might have had an answer that night, but I hadn't discerned who was trying to get my attention. If we want God to visit or speak His wisdom to us, then we must be ready when He initiates it. We can't hesitate or we will miss it.

Evangelist Smith Wigglesworth was someone who acted upon what God said at the drop of a hat. Because of that, he was known as a man of great faith. He didn't doubt God. That is one of the traits I saw in Jesus as He walked the Earth. He always heard from the Father and acted right away upon what He heard. He never hesitated. If the Lord speaks to you, you have to act on it right away.

God said to John, "Come up higher." John said, "I heard a great voice." He was able to describe the hair, feet, voice, clothing, and everything about our Lord, including how beautiful He was.

God wants us to come up to that higher place, the glory realm. The next big movement in the church will be the glory realm. There is a lot of angelic movement there. You will feel angelic movements all around you. You will also realize that you are in a place where you hear from God far more easily than you ever have before.

GLORY HIGHWAY

(*Sister Ruth now shares more of her story.*) I want to share some wonderful events that God has done in my life. The Word says, "Prepare ye the way." The road to Heaven is straight and narrow. There is only room for you and for Jesus on that road. The narrow road is good. It's so wonderful!

Please allow God to put His road map into your heart and spirit so that you can move with Him. He tells us, "Go ye into all the world, and preach the gospel" (Mark 16:15 KJV). The plans He has summon all who read the Word.

God isn't limited. He isn't looking at your education. He isn't looking at what you don't have or don't know. He knows it all. Be guided by the Spirit and by the plan and purpose of God. You will be able to do more than what you have considered or have even thought about.

He said by the Spirit that we don't know what He has for us. His Spirit will release it to us. He said, "I know the plans I have for you" (Jeremiah 29:11). These things haven't come into our mind or our heart. He will cause it to come into your spirit. He will release it to you. His Spirit will reap what He has sown in you.

The Lord will show you that His ways are great and that He is greatly to be praised (Psalm 96:4). Praise Him. Summon Him. Come into His courts with thanksgiving and with praise. Come with joy and with celebration. Come into the quietness and good-ness of the Lord. Come into the being of the Lord. He will give you your passport to "Go ye into all the world to preach the gos-pel" (Mark 16:15).

He said that few find this narrow road, this high way where the blessings and the goodness are. You want to find the Lord's blessings and goodness. You want to find what He is doing and have a life full of His goodness. You will live in the knowledge that whatever you ask of God, He is more than able to work.

You won't mind a little training. All soldiers are forever being trained. If you are in His army, the training never ends. You are always training for bigger things and larger territories. There are bigger battles, greater weapons, higher levels of understanding, and more to possess in God.

This is what you want. You want to learn of Him daily. You will be crying more than you will be laughing because you will be weeping over the goodness of the Lord and what He can do for you.

Day by day, you will see the glorious report of the Lord. Many times, God won't share every detail with you ahead of time because of the preparation that is involved. Sometimes the sched-ule will change. You may come to that turning point in your life that depends upon your decision of wanting to know and follow God.

Your strength will come. Joy is coming in the morning. The new day is here and we are going to be in the A.M. service. He is the I AM. We are going to be in the I AM service of the Lord. I AM whatever You need me to be or You want to accomplish. He is ready to care for you.

I have been in some strange situations where God has rescued me. One day, I fell asleep at the wheel of my car. I drove for half a mile in the city, sound asleep! I woke up when a car horn blew. I was about to go through a red light.

God said to me, "I am with you always, even unto the end of the world" (Matthew 28:20 KJV). I am not suggesting that you pray with your eyes closed or drive when you are tired. I am just telling you that His eye is on the sparrow. His eye is upon you. He is continually keeping you, charging you, and pouring into you every day.

You will hear His voice in little conversations that you over-hear. You will turn on the television and suddenly, a prophetic word will come. You will hear someone speak one or two words, and you know it's for you. It's easy to hear the voice of the Lord, the Spirit of the Lord. He will say, "Go this way."

Once, a few people were trying to lay a trap for me. I didn't know it at the time, but they were testing my spirituality. I was sent on an errand in China, where everything was in Chinese.

They put me on a bus. I didn't know that the bus was going to return to that same circle. I thought, *Well, if we go home, we might as well go home from China.* The Lord said the word "entrapment." He didn't think it was a very nice thing that the people were doing to me.

When I finally got off of the bus, the Lord said to me, "Don't go to the left where you are to meet the person. Go to the right." He was protecting me. That doesn't mean that He disliked the person, but God is all about righteousness and truth. And He was planning to bail me out of this trap because I was innocent.

I came up behind the people who were waiting for me to return from my "errand." They were looking in another direction. I remember hitting the back of their car with my hand as I said, "What are you doing?"

They began to laugh and laugh. They said, "Oh, you caught us! Now we know that you are spiritual!" Do you understand the story? Everything about you will be tried in the light of His glory. Who you are will be tried in the gold of Heaven.

What God is doing in you isn't for today or tomorrow. It's for eternity. That means everything. It doesn't matter how small or great or how minute you think things are. God will have His mind, His Spirit, and His thoughts in us so that our days will be full of glory for His name's sake.

You know, God catches fish in a net. He has a special net for you. He has a special way of capturing you, captivating you, and getting you into the place where He can deposit into your life. He gives you the words, revelations, and mysteries of who you are and who He is. He gives you knowledge of the divine undertaking of your calling. It's a divine thing. Never let that slip your mind. It's the divine character, nature, and person of Christ in you and the hope of all glory.

No man can gainsay how you have been mentored. The way you have walked is opposite. It's in another direction from many others. You want to see past the darkness, and you will. Be the person God is calling you to be. Be the testimony of what He speaks.

Hear what God is speaking to His church. We won't fall away. We won't be like so many who straddle the fence of who they are. Don't even get on that fence. Let Him fence you into His purposes. Be that person who knows their God. You will do exploits. Your life will be a life of wonderful surprises. Most of all, your life will have the unusual, the unknown, and the indivisible of who God is.

What is hidden is coming under the brightness of His glory. Your light will dissipate the darkness. And when God gives you a vision, a knowing, or even a doctrine, no one can take it away from you. Don't be surprised if you sometimes start out with very little. God does great things with the little.

When I traveled with Sister Ruth, she would tell me, "Ruth, just bring a little." I asked, "How much is a little?" We stayed in England. She had told me to bring a suit. I had one suit and two blouses for six weeks. We traveled light because we needed the suitcase. There was only a hand suitcase to carry all of the brochures and bulletins.

After a while, you realize something. It's not I that is living here. It's Christ occupying here. We experience the glory when we learn how to walk away from the things of the world. As Brother Kevin says, we experienced the glory because we learned how to walk away from the things of the world. That's not really taught a lot today.

We traveled all over the British Isles for six weeks. Sister Ruth Heflin spoke four times a day. The Lord had said, "I want you to go to England and declare liberty." He allowed Sister Ruth to learn that John Kennedy had planted a plaque in one of the garden parks. It's a metal or iron plaque about England having liberty.

We went out one day in the rain just to find it. We went declaring liberty as far north and as far south as you could go. Sister Ruth preached on the knowledge of the glory of the Lord covering the Earth.

We had a measure of liberty when we traveled. We never worried about finances even when we had no money. God always gave more than what was needed. Don't be concerned over where you will stay or where you are going. Just study the Lord before you go.

Sister Ruth always came with a vision for every country we traveled in. I remember when we arrived in the British Isles. She only had change in her purse and I didn't have any money. When we met our host, Sister Ruth reached into her purse as if she was reaching for the fare. I held my breath. Suddenly, the man said, "Oh, let me do this, Sister Ruth." Our host paid for our fare.

Another time, it was the hottest summer on record. We spent a day and a half there, at a cost of fifteen thousand pounds. That's about twenty thousand dollars. That's a lot of money. Someone paid our entire bill. God covered the bill. When God covers the bill, He gives you a thrill! Hallelujah! He takes care of everything. We were ladies and lords moving in the plan of God.

You know, the queen has to travel with many trucks. We are kings who are bringing in the train load. We are bringing in the glory. The Bible says that we are kings and priests. There are blessings in the glory. Get that in your mind and spirit. He wants to multiply and bless you.

Brother Kevin tells us that nothing is wasted in God, not even a crumb or a piece of bread. The Word says that when the Lord fed the multitudes, they gathered up twelve baskets of crumbs. There is more than enough in the glory.

Traveling with Sister Heflin was a daily experience. We went to Australia and to Europe. We went through fifteen European countries. I stayed in Israel for twenty-eight years. It takes the wealth of God to be able to do that. We didn't have the finances.

I didn't know that part of my calling was to minister to the Jewish people and to seek the Jews out in the Earth. We went into every synagogue and community center to invite the Jews to go home to Israel. While we were in Israel, the Lord told us, "As long as you have your worship services here, war will never come to Israel." That word from the Lord was a sign to us.

Fall in love with God's love. Be part of what God is doing in Israel. If you want to walk in the glory, then let Israel be a priority in your life. Strengthen her. Bless her. Study her to know what she likes and what she is all about. Stand for Israel and God will do the same for you.

You will know, without any doubt in your heart, what God is doing and how He is moving in the Earth. He does things overnight. While we sleep, He brings light. The light has come and the glory of the Lord is about to shine upon Israel. Get involved with her. Let a birthing come.

When we traveled, Sister Ruth always treated me royally, but she would never tell me what was about to happen. We could be at prayer. Then she would say, "Ruth, you are going to speak in the next five minutes."

I have learned that if you are going to speak, *pray a lot in tongues.* Don't try to find a sermon. Speak in tongues. Your prayer language is so important. You won't necessarily know what you are praying, but the Holy Ghost will stir up exactly what you need. And He will give you the words to speak when you need them. This is how we learned. The river began to flow.

I am sharing these things because you need to know. You want to hear what God is giving you. It's new to your ears. It's going into your heart and your belly. You are studying the ways of the Lord. They are past finding out (Romans 11:33). Just when you think you have learned something, He says, "No, there is something over here. There is more over here."

Pray In Tongues without ceasing And Be Thankful

God has to get our full attention. He does this beautifully in the *Song of Solomon.* He says, "Come away, My love. Come away. Winter is past. The rain has stopped. The flowers are blooming. The birds are singing and there is the sound of the turtle in the land."

God is looking for that sound in us. It's a sound that will possess the land, the nations, and the countries. It's time for us to be on the jury. I'm not talking about judging people for their worth. We are to judge what God is doing. He is doing a brand-new thing. This is the "high way" that the Word of God says that we are to find (Numbers 21:22).

When I was innocent and probably ignorant, I thought there was a *highway* out there. So I would look up at the sky. Any way you say it, God was leading me toward it. He said that anyone who comes onto it will know. We won't be ignorant.

We will know the high way. There won't be any negativity on that high way. However, there are some things that keep us from knowing it and walking on it. God doesn't work amidst bitterness, strife, or anger. *God works in the joy of looking toward the prize.*

He works in us when we look toward what He is bringing about and when we actively become a part of it. You want to get on that high way. The high way is straight. It's moving with God.

We want to awaken every day with whatever the Lord wants to say to us. We want His words in our heart and mind. Don't think of the high way as something you won't be able to handle. God will prepare you to handle all that He asks you to do. He will give you a quick vision or glance at what He is preparing. He does this so that you will know what to do when it begins to happen.

You know, the Israelites went through a lot of travels and a lot of battles. Their road wasn't an easy one. Many of them died in the wilderness. The roads we travel aren't always smooth. When we travel through the tough places, we see the glory of the Lord moving throughout the journey.

The Lord has a treasure that money can't buy. His wealth of revelation is going to carry you every place in life that you need to go. It will carry you into every position and set you before every person. He can do this because He is the King of kings. When you meet Him, you can face anyone. You can weather the storms.

Let people see Christ in you, without announcing it. They will discern that something is different. Let the King come in, in full measure and full stature. You won't be looking without knowing or seeing. You will have the assurance that, "This is God. This is the path." Walk in it with confidence.

God is moving in the places where we see kings and priests in the church. He isn't just appearing in His robes. He is giving appointments, messages, and directions. He is bringing change to the body. He will reveal who He is and who we are meant to be in Him.

YIELD TO ME

(*Sister Ruth continues her story.*) It is important not to limit the Lord or what He can do. He knows where everything is. He is constantly taking down, repairing, and building anew. Let me give you a few more sparks that will ignite you. You know, a story has to be a testimony of all that God does, or it isn't the testimony of Jesus. I'm just telling you. There may be some anointing there, but what you really want is the *testimony*.

The Bible says that everywhere Jesus went, He was doing good. He healed a multitude. He raised the dead. He healed the sick everywhere. Yet because of people's faith, in some places He wasn't able to do much. I don't want to miss it. I want it all.

People have to draw God to themselves. Don't wait for others to single you out. Don't pray until other people hear you. Draw them to the fire that is within you. Draw them to the fireplace burning inside of you. Sometimes God will just take you and spread you throughout the nations. That's what happened to me.

One day, I was thinking about Israel. I read in the Old Testament where it says, "I passed by you and I saw you polluted in your own blood. I picked you up and washed you off and put jewels on you" (Ezekiel 16:6-13).

I was asked to attend a funeral on a Sunday, which was unusual in Virginia, where we lived at the time. I believe that the people were Jewish. Their traditions dictated that the person was to be buried on the same day. I said that I would go to the funeral.

On the way there, I felt a little sting in my belly. When we arrived at the little chapel, I didn't feel very comfortable, so I sat in the sanctuary. Sister Ruth Heflin was doing the eulogy. At some point, I excused myself to go to the bathroom. All of a sudden, I found all of my blood running out of my body—all of it! It ran out in the way that water runs from a spigot. A blood vessel broke. I won't go into the condition.

Four times in four months, I had heard the Lord tell me, "You shall not die in your own blood, but live." In fact, a few days before the funeral, Sister Ruth and I were in North Dakota. On the way to the platform to preach, the Lord said to Sister Ruth, "Yield to Me."

I love the way that God moves. Sister Ruth replied, "Lord, I thought I was yielding." But the Lord said again, "Yield to Me." Sister Ruth began to hear the song, "And the dead shall be raised. The blind shall see and the deaf shall hear." When we returned to Virginia, she gave her testimony. I listened to her give it. I should have listened more closely, because God was speaking about me.

You have to catch things in your spirit. It's as if the spotlight is upon you. It's a revelation just for you. It's a better movie than you will ever see in the world. Movies aren't a thrill for me. I saw the moving existence of God in living color. That's how I learned of the glory. I saw Him in color.

I couldn't figure out why the Lord only showed me that image once. Later when He came with more glory, He said, "I kept you for five years with that one vision." I waited all that time. You have to wait on the Lord. Time redeems everything.

Although I was bleeding heavily, I somehow managed to get out of the church bathroom beneath the sanctuary. By the time I climbed the stairs, the funeral was over. Suddenly, I fell to the floor. The people there were so spiritual. They thought I fell out under the power of the Holy Spirit, so they just left me there!

Finally, my niece, who had come to the funeral with me, told Sister Ruth that I had passed out. Sister Ruth soon realized that I hadn't passed out. I had *passed on*. Sister Ruth began to hear the same song in her spirit that she had heard in North Dakota.

She picked me up in her arms and had someone carry me into a side room. There she placed me in her lap and put my feet on a chair. She began to sing over me, "And the dead shall be raised. The blind shall see and the deaf shall hear in My glory."

She sung that song over me until I came back to life. I was deceased for about fifteen minutes. But remember that the Lord had told me, "You shall not die in your own blood, but live." God had plans for me! He has plans for you.

My hip had been out of joint and the pain was terrible. Apparently I took too much medicine, which caused a blood vessel to break. I lost all of my blood except for a few pints. Sister Ruth began to pray for me until I could get medical attention. I regained consciousness in the ambulance on the way to the hospital.

I heard someone say that they wanted to monitor me. They were planning to cut off my dress. I guess I became "female" all of a sudden. I don't know what happened, but I said, "Don't cut this dress off of me!" The paramedic said, "What?" They thought I was still unconscious. I said, "I haven't paid for this dress yet. Don't cut it off!"

The paramedic said, "What do you want me to do with it?" And I said, "Unbutton it, silly!" You know, that didn't sound very nice, but in the state I was in, I knew that I hadn't paid for the dress. It cost a little money. I still had it on my credit card!

Don't you know that despite everything that got on that dress, it all came out in the wash? I'm throwing this in for a little humor, because some people "lose it" when things don't go the right way. They would just throw the "dress" away. Don't do that if there is something left that can be redeemed.

At the hospital, a missionary took care of me. In the emergency room, he told me what he thought had happened. I said, "Brother, I believe you have a word of knowledge." He said, "Yes, I'm a missionary from the islands."

The doctor came to see me. He kept saying bad words. I finally told him to stop saying those words. We don't want to give the devil any honor. I told him, "Don't say that anymore. I won't have it."

That doctor came back to me three times, trying to figure out what had happened to me. I talked to him at length. I even spoke a little about spiritual things. At one point, I saw two angels in the room. I also had a visitor, who brought a box of candy. I'm not a candy eater, but God was telling me that I would live to eat that candy.

When I finally returned home, a friend came to visit. She told me a story about a person she had been with that day, while I was going through my ordeal. She said, "I want you to help me pray for this doctor's wife." It was the wife of the doctor who had taken care of me in the hospital.

God was doing many things that day. He got Sister Ruth Heflin involved. He got the doctor involved. The angels were involved. The people coming to visit me were involved. This all happened, but the Lord had said, "You shall not die in your own blood, but live." It was quite an ordeal!

You know, I didn't want any of that to happen. We all want to be super strong like everyone else who is with us. We think that when we are weak, we don't have faith at work, but God is working faith out in all that He does. Allow Him to pierce your heart. Let Him pierce everything. When His blood flows, it brings healing. Let the blood of Jesus be there to heal so you become more like Him.

You might be in the belly of the whale right now, but you will come out! Jonah didn't want to go where God sent him. He kept going down, down and down. When we go down, God lifts up His standard. He performs His Word and brings forth what He has ordained for your life. When He touches you, you will never be the same.

I now live in Arizona. That's probably because one day, I said to the Lord, "Lord, when You move in the last days, I don't care where it is or what country it's in or even what city. I don't care who it's with. I want to be in the middle of it." You have to make some challenges with the Lord. I awoke one morning and told Him that I needed something new. He responded with two words. He said, "Phoenix, Arizona." Two minutes later, I got a phone call about Phoenix.

The Lord knows where the person is that we need to talk to. I heard the person ask, "How would you like to go to Phoenix?" They simply wanted me to come. They didn't know I had just received a word from the Lord.

Another word had already been given that a great move of God was going to be in America, beginning in Phoenix. The person on the phone now told me that she had some land in Arizona. She asked if I would like to come and look at it. I thought, *Do I want to go to Arizona just to look at a piece of land?* But I said that I would go, because the woman had mentored me and blessed me. She was one of my spiritual mothers. Two days later, Sister Ruth suddenly asked me, "How would you like to go to Arizona?" These two ladies were worlds apart!

Sister Ruth had several meetings already set up. All of the big pastors from Phoenix came to the meetings. We had a three-day period of laughter. We just laughed and laughed. God opened a door. As I prepared to leave from there, a friend asked, "Do you think you will ever live in Phoenix?" I said, "Well, I don't know." Do we ever know?

A few days later, I was ministering with Sister Ruth in another city and I had a kidney attack. I was nearly unconscious, with a temperature of one hundred and six degrees. I was going to board a plane that night and return home because I was so sick.

At the service, Sister Ruth walked up to me and asked, "Are you too sick to lead the music?" I said, "No." So she said, "All right. Lead the music before you go home." When I got up to lead the music, everything before me was a blur. I could hardly see because my temperature was so high. Then I saw the back doors open. They led straight down the aisle to the pulpit.

Next, I saw the Lord ride in on a big white horse! He was dressed in white. His stirrups had turquoise on them. There was a big piece of turquoise on a gold chain hanging across the horse's nose. That was a beautiful sight, but what was He saying? I'm telling you that when you agree with God and work with Him, He will lead you into His plan and purpose for your life.

I was standing at the pulpit. I could hardly see Him, but He said, "Will you ride with Me?" Those were His words. Of course my answer was, "God, sure." This happened about two months before I moved to Phoenix. For me, the turquoise was the key, because you can find turquoise in Arizona.

I thought about the vision for a while. The Lord didn't prophesy or speak to me in a dream. He caught me at a bad moment. I was so sick that I could hardly see. He was concerned about my health. He sure got my attention! Many times, God does things to stop everything up. He turns our attention solely to Him so that we will understand His plan.

I have seen my life go into places that money could never afford. I would never have been able to go if I hadn't followed into the rough and difficult places. Those were the places of saying "Yes" when I wanted to say "No." Those were places where I wanted to run. They were places where I was living a horrible lifestyle and where I said, "If I will just get saved, I'll have a better life."

There will be rough places in life even after we are saved. There will be that bump in the road, like when the wrong man touched the Ark. We want to touch God in a way that the glory that was on the Ark will enter our life. The Ark brings in the gold and the silver. It brings in the precious things. I'm not talking about natural things. I'm talking about things that are spiritual and everlasting—from glory to glory.

We look for teachings on all of the great things and we can have those. It's all about learning who God is and identifying Him and moving with Him. Move with God. Move with His plan and purpose and hasten the Lord's return.

He is moving more quickly today. He is going to move with honor. He will move in a way that will make others jealous. He told me that. He said, "I'm going to make others jealous by putting the glory on some people because they want to know Me and Me only."

Do you want to know the "I AM"? How many of you want that? He is the I AM. Let's endure the little things and the hard things. Yield your spirit and soul to the Lord. Totally yield every member of yourself to Him. Yield your seeing, hearing, talking, and every place you travel to Him.

Go to the right places. Spend your money at the right places. The Lord told me, "Don't look for things. I will create them for you. Don't waste your time finding things. I will get them for you. I will have the right people there. I am way ahead of you. Before you were born, I was working out your plan."

Be real with the Lord. Tell Him things you need to tell Him. Don't keep them inside. Open up. Say, "Lord, I have this situation. Please work on it." Right away, He will put you into this explosive place where you will wonder what is happening.

It is the Lord's doing. It is the Lord's works. It's the Lord's way of operating. Let Him do it and you will share your experiences forever with others who are around you. Be blessed and be a blessing to the Lord.

STEPPING IN

This is Kevin, friends. As you can see, there is a very real personality and character side of Jesus that He wants us to move into. He has many sides, like facets in a diamond. The riches of His glory are going to shine in us.

He wants us to understand, illustrate, and manifest what He is doing in the heavens. That day will come and now is (John 4:23). You can feel it. You won't know whether you are in or out of the Spirit. The natural man and the spiritual man will be working together.

You will know when you aren't operating in the Spirit. You'll know it without question. Right now, a lot of people are wandering and searching instead of knowing. God wants you to know that He is always with you and He is always doing something new.

He said it's a new day. It's now. "Shall ye not know it? Shall it not break forth on the right and on the left?" (Isaiah 54:3). You will live in a different atmosphere. It's not the same as yesterday. It's never the same. It never repeats itself. There is more to God. You will see more and more of Him. You will understand His nature, His ways, His presence, and His character.

We begin to be like Him, to look like Him, and to serve like Him. This is His promise in His Word. He said, "As I am with My Father, you also will be with Me" (John 17:21). You will know Me. You will understand My ways that are very high. Now let's listen in as Sister Ruth reveals a little more of her story.

(*Sister Ruth's testimony continues.*) Saints, sometimes we get a little glimpse of the glory, but it seems elusive. God sort of dangles it out there like a carrot. I have seen this several times. It pulls back but it is designed to draw us nearer to Him.

I was searching for the glory. I was hungry to see into the invisible, hidden, and secret places where the Lord works. He spoke some profound things to my heart as I searched. He said, "If you will follow Me, if you submit yourself, if you will take up your cross." He used the words, "Take up your cross and follow Me."

Some of those zones looked very dangerous. I didn't really want to walk into some of those areas because they were so unknown. I thought I might miss the glory. We are like that. We think that way. We think we might miss it.

You won't. You will have light everywhere you can see. God will make sure that you can see. He will anoint your eyes to see and your ears to hear. He will anoint you in your spirit, so you will know what He is doing.

It's a new thing He is bringing into the Earth. It's the next realm. We are going to move into the knowledge of the glory of the ways of the Lord in all the Earth. This glory will be everywhere. *Step into it.*

When you come into the glory, it will bring you into a new state of knowing. It's like having an understanding that was always there but is only now being revealed to you. Sometimes, what you know or speak will take you by surprise. You are going to be speaking with authority. Learn to use the authority that is within you.

Once when I was taking an offering, a pastor wrote on a big piece of paper. He held it in front of me. It said, "Speak with authority." Speak from the heavens. Speak from God's heart. The timing of everything is in His heart. That heart beats passionately for you and for me to know Him.

A great prophet of God said to me, "Lift your voice." The voice that you hear when I speak is my normal voice. I don't know how to speak at any other level. It's at the level of anointing that God has given me.

When you speak, your voice will cause the enemies of your soul to flee in seven directions. They won't stand the power God imparts upon you to bring a release. It will bring forth thirty, sixty, or a hundredfold into your life, so speak with authority. When you know Him, you have His authority working in you.

Paul said, "Oh, that I might know Him" (Philippians 3:10). He didn't know the places that he would stay, the road he would walk, or the places he would journey into. We are stepping into a new way of knowing God. We'll speak with power.

Speak what God entrusts to you and what He deposits in your life. This is what pulls us after Him. There is something more, something else. Declare it. Pull it from the heavens every day. We can't study. What God did ten minutes ago, He's now doing *right now*. Have you thought about that?

Brother Kevin reveals that he thinks about this all of the time. He says that we need to get people to understand this because they get into a rut or a system so that it's predictable. He says that God is predictable about His Word and His truth. He establishes truth, but His ways are His personality. Jesus healed in different ways. Sometimes He ministered to people who needed deliverance, but in different ways. He just never stuck to one thing.

He says that people think there are certain ways that are established to "do" it and to enter in. But this move of God started a couple of years ago. It's a new thing that became more evident as of January first of this year.

But now we will have a new sound, a new song, and a different angle of seeing the ways of the Lord. They are past your natural mind, but your spirit understands. He said, "My Spirit will show you what I am doing in these days."

One morning, I was preparing to go to church. I remember the moment, even the time of day. A word came out of me in a whisper. It was as if the Lord was speaking. It wasn't me. He was ushering in more glory. I said, "Lord, would You have me under the shadow of Your wings today?" I wasn't thinking of anything terrible or what might happen that day. I just felt this closeness of God that I had never experienced before.

As soon as I went into the church, the glory caught me halfway between the front and the back. It hit me as I came down the aisle. I said, "Something's happening." You have to recognize the glory and declare it. You should get a little excited about it! It's worth much more than money or even gold. The glory is the preciousness of Jesus!

I dropped my purse and my Bible onto the seat and ran up to one of the heads of the church. I said, "Something is happening in this place!" You know, sometimes we wait too long and the glory passes us by. We have to grab it quickly because it's a moment the Lord has given to us.

I said to one of the people there, "God is answering prayers. Something is happening! It's happening! Don't you feel it?" I said this two or three times. "It's here! It's here!" The Holy Spirit laid me out on the floor. I felt the pillars of His smoke go through me. It ran to me and back, like waves on a shoreline.

Right now, we are in the waves of His glory. That is what the Lord told me. He is sending glory waves. He is taking us out and back in again. These are baptisms we have never experienced before. Every time He takes us out, He removes the old and deposits the new. It's all brand new. When a woman buys a new dress, by the end of the day, it's no longer new. The glory is new all day long, every day. Brother Kevin knows what I'm talking about.

I saw great miracles and moves that Sister Heflin had in God. I saw the awesome ways of God. Many pastors would send for her.

Sometimes she had to say "No" because they weren't prepared for the higher things. You have to be prepared for the glory. Moving in the presence of the Lord is so real. You can't get around it.

At times, there seemed to be a depth of water in front of me. I would ask, "Am I going through it? Do I have to be baptized in it? Lord, what are You showing me?" I kept trying to lift my feet to step over a spiritual pool. The water was going around and around. It was up to my waist, like when Ezekiel saw that river. There are levels of God. You start out in ankle-deep water. You can't run very far in ankle-deep water. By the time it gets knee-deep, you can hardly walk! The glory comes in waves.

God wants to take us to the level where His government is upon us. That's the way of the cloud, the way of the Spirit, the way of the heavenlies. It comes by waiting on the Lord and by committing everything unto Him.

We are at a time when we are to reach out with our faith and say, "Lord, spring it upon me. Surprise me. Let me enjoy who You are. Let me recognize who You are." God uses His newness to sharpen us. Eternity is coming in. He is restoring our youth like an eagle. You will see it.

The Lord taught me how to travel. When you move in the glory, you travel lightly. You may think that you have to take a lot with you. We think we need these things. Ladies are famous for this. You take the biggest suitcase you can find. Believe me, it will really limit you from moving for God.

One of the first things the Lord told me when preparing to travel was, "I don't want you spending time in the shops, looking.

I will have everything you need at hand. I will create it. I will have it there." God taught me. I can tell you some funny stories.

The weight of the glory is like a train. That's how it moves. The sound of a train is the glory coming in, whether you are ready or not. You are going to climb aboard the glory train. We can feel the glory invade our privacy, our thoughts, and all that we do. We can even feel the checkpoints that lead up to the station—that point in time when the glory train arrives. And we can feel every checkpoint even after it has departed the station (so to speak).

In the glory, you may lose track of time. When Sister Ruth Heflin would begin to minister, it was as if we had been there for only a few moments. One day we sang for six hours. She walked into the tabernacle and picked up the microphone. We usually had other people leading, but that day she just picked up the microphone and began singing.

We knew we were standing on holy ground because she was manifesting and transcribing what God was doing at that moment. We knew God was preparing for greater things that were yet to come. God prepares for everything and meets all of our needs. I realize now that we never owed anyone anything.

(*Kevin now shares his thoughts.*) There are hidden treasures everywhere. It takes eyes to see and ears to hear to know what the Holy Spirit is saying. God speaks in the least likely places and brings supernatural provision, such as things that will happen that didn't seem as if they would.

There is a life of victory and fulfillment in the glory realm, but people today aren't routinely taught to deny themselves. When you walk away from the selfishness that this world encourages you to live in, you begin to encounter the treasures of Heaven. That's where you find true victory and fulfillment.

When we deny ourselves and carry our own cross, wonderful things occur. The most powerful visitations of God are during those times when it seems as if we give away more than we receive. We don't seem to have a will or control of our life, because the Lord is leading.

For example, I wanted to break a fast, so I went somewhere to get a meal. While I carried it out, the Lord said, "Sow it to a street person." He put me back on the fast. He was developing the way I was moving with Him.

At times, I have felt a bit like Elijah and Elisha (2 Kings 2). The promise was that if Elisha stayed with Elijah until the very end, Elisha would get the mantle. I saw Elijah at the end there. He was trying to lose Elisha. He said, "I'm going to go to Bethel. You stay here in Jericho." He would just keep going, but Elisha would say, "No, I'm going to stay with you."

What did Elijah say to Elisha when he wanted his spirit? He said, "You are asking for a hard thing." When he went after him, he wasn't ready to go. He had a few other things he wanted to do.

Sister Ruth has shared that she has encountered some of the same things. She had to be ready at a moment's notice. She calls it a moment of eternity. She can tell you that it was difficult at first because she didn't want it naturally in the flesh. Let's look at more of her testimony.

(*Sister Ruth's story now continues.*) I can say that I have done a few things. I can speak about the hard things because I'm a great-grandmother. I have raised multitudes of children in the Spirit.

I have lived in seventy-five nations. I have built churches, hospitals, and orphanages. I have lived in Australia, the Philippines, China, Africa, Russia, and all over Europe. I traveled the trains of Europe for three months, through fifteen nations.

I have been before many great people, including many presidents. I ministered to three or four presidents and other people in high places. I really wasn't looking for any of that. I didn't ask for it.

It didn't matter to me whether I went or not. I do know that it matters to God. He is looking for people who will be a voice of the Spirit, a voice of the clouds. He wants us to speak things into existence that are not yet (Hebrews 11:1). That is our faith working. We are going to give some things away by faith. We are going to speak things forth by faith. It will stretch us. At first, it will make us a little uncomfortable. Then things will become easier.

I have found that every time I wanted to come into a new level, there was a time of waiting, fasting, and change. There was also a time of sacrifice. As we change seasons, we begin to get rid of things that make us comfortable. They really aren't God's comfort. We let go of precious things that aren't what the Lord wants.

Sometimes God will separate you from your dearest friends or family. You may move to another church. Don't go unless He moves you. Don't be a wanderer. Let God move you into that new place. The Lord brings change. It's a kind of change where you aren't the same person today that you were yesterday or last week. He begins to remove the encumbrances and hindrances that keep us from the higher places.

Often when we traveled, natural conveniences were missing. We learned not to worry about the little things. There are personal stories concerning the sacrifices we make that only Heaven will reveal. A life of sacrifice seems to come with the glory. Giving is sacrificial. It has to hurt a little to make a difference to how we believe and live.

Some people seem to do things so easily. Some men and women of God have so much joy! Why are they so happy? They have found the key. They have tapped into the glory. That's why they have such great strength to do the work of the Lord. They have an ongoing, uncompromising ministry. The blessing is always there in the glory.

They don't stop and start. They move onward because they obeyed the Lord in so many little areas. Some are areas that don't seem important to most people. With God, even the little is part of the picture.

One day, the Lord spoke to me. He said, "I want My people to be grateful for what I did for them." You have to know the ways of the Lord and respond. Give thanks and praise in everything. You will find yourself dancing, being silly, being foolish, and just clapping your hands. It's the joy of the Lord. You are responding to the Lord. You aren't bashful or ashamed. These are little keys that the Lord has shown me.

One day I complained a little about some of the hard knocks. I was complaining about a little cross, a little difficulty that I was carrying. The Lord showed me how "big" my cross really was. It was hardly big enough to put around my neck, if you know what I mean!

He wanted me to go somewhere that was a difficult place. I knew it was difficult. I knew there were drugs and adultery and things you don't want to talk about. God had someone call me to see if I would go. I said, "Yes," thinking the person wouldn't call me back. They were like that. You may know people who are that way. They call and then forget to call again for ten years.

I fasted on water for seven days and hoped the person wouldn't call again. On the seventh day, I thought, *Lord, I don't mind going, but I really don't want to go.* I was being double-minded. You can't be double-minded about anything. Just do it. Let God get rid of your flesh. Let everything be of Him.

On the seventh day, I thought that the man wouldn't call back. I thought, *He just won't,* but he did. His first words were, "Are you coming?" I couldn't get out of going. I really wrestled with it. I got down on my knees and prayed again. I said, "Jesus, I really don't want to go out there. I really don't." I knew there would be fire, wind, and hail. It is in the weather reports that really get to you that you will see what God is doing. Brother Kevin says that it comes with the territory.

People are concerned about these things. They have to deal with all of these little tragedies, but that is part of being in the Kingdom. I remember the Lord asking, "Do you want to follow Me? Take up your cross."

Many times, I hear people complain about their sufferings. Listen. If you suffer with Him, you are going to reign with Him. You are going to know Him. He wants us to know Him. Know that He is always with you, even to the ends of the Earth. Let Him speak that into your heart.

I have had visions of people who have little crosses around their necks. We don't want to wear them around our neck. We want them in our heart, in our movements, and in our dealings with others. We are to prefer others first. We are to give them the bigger portions. We offer them the best because we are servants. We are part of the living creatures of how God moves in *Ezekiel*.

Pentecost was in *Ezekiel* before it ever got into the Book of *Acts*. Ezekiel saw the fire of the Lord. He saw the plan, the hand, and the ways of the Lord. If you want to move with God, then learn of His ways. He said, "My ways are high." His purposes are always going somewhere.

If we will follow God, we will have a good life. Many people in the church already believe that they have a good life. They really have a mediocre life. They never get to the place where they have total freedom and victory in the Lord.

Of course, there are exceptions. The first time I saw one young man's face, it had such beauty upon it that I wanted to weep. I thought, *I know this brother from somewhere.* I wanted to ask, "Brother, do I know you from somewhere?" We knew each other by the Spirit. He had a look upon his face that told me he treats his mother and his wife well.

I could tell that he handles things with a good spirit. I just knew these things by the look that was on his face. I could see that he has looked into the face of the Lord and that everything is okay. Everything is good between them. These are just the little matters.

There is more to come and more to understand. There is more reality in the Lord. He wants to show you His ways and how He operates. He wants to put the blessing on all you prepare.

Allow God to touch you in the areas that are weak and that you withhold for yourself. Open up and you will be wise, well, ready, and healthier than ever. You will be available for the work of the Lord. You will be on time and you won't miss a thing.

You will know when to speak and when not to speak. And you will know that you know. There will be a knowing inside of you. You will know the ways of the Lord. The anointing of the Lord will be upon you to do wonderful and great exploits for the Lord. You won't live from a fleshly perspective. What we know will soon disappear. We are learning how to glean from the heavens to live in the ease of the glory. Now, that's a train you really want to catch.

Five

GLORY TRAIN

God, give us that earnestness right now in our heart to run after You. You said, draw Me and I'll run after you. Lord, that we will run after You. Let our thinking, our standards, and our schedules change. Let there be change in our hearts to come after You. Let purpose come. Let us be a purpose-driven people, Lord—not from a book, but from Your book. We're here to occupy.

Lord, in the natural, we raise children. We plant fields and gardens. Lord, You planted a seed in us that will bring a whole forest forward in these last days. God, the leaves of the trees will be healing for the nations. We thank You, we love You, we know You, we will follow You, and we bless You, in the holy name of Your precious Son, Jesus. Amen.

—SISTER RUTH CARNEAL

UTTERMOST REGIONS

Saints, Sister Ruth has given us a great overview of the glory, as well as some of the more finite aspects, hasn't she? As believers, we are commanded to preach the *Good News* gospel unto the uttermost regions of the Earth. Preaching the gospel to the whole world isn't only about pulpits and reciting Scripture verses. It's so much more.

Can you tell that God is preparing to return the church to the Book of *Acts*? It's true. We are returning to the days when the Holy Spirit first fell upon the corporate body.

We can read in *Acts 1:2* that Jesus gave commandments to His disciples through the Holy Spirit. Jesus speaks by His Holy Spirit from the throne of glory. His voice and His power reach down through the glory to transform nations.

He is looking upon, preparing, and healing nations. He is measuring. He is studying nations to see who will measure up and who will support Israel. He is seeking those who will be fair and just with her. He said, "Son of man, you have the measuring line" (Ezekiel 40:3). We need to measure what God is doing.

Jesus and His disciples traveled everywhere sharing the good news and performing miraculous works of salvation, healing, and deliverance. We are likewise commanded to go into the world and do the works He did—and greater works (John 14:12).

Our testimony of God's goodness continues this work by transforming the lives of those who hear and believe our stories. Jesus said that the works the Father gave Him to finish bear witness that He was sent (John 5:36). We are sent ones who are here to do the works of the Lord.

Touching the glory transforms an ordinary testimony into one that opens the eyes of those who walk in physical and spiritual darkness. Our witness demonstrates how God moves people out of darkness into the light of an extraordinary and eternal future. If you don't think your life is extraordinary, you don't yet see the glory working in you and in the lives of those you encounter.

The good news is that the day of glory is here! Invite the Lord into your life and fully surrender to Him. Once you step into His glory realm, all you see and do becomes a celebration of the Lord. You begin to look, think, and act like Him. He enables you to see others as integral members of the body of Christ, which allows you to minister with His compassion and love.

When we share our stories with the broken and lost, they can see God's light of truth in us. We become a beacon in the darkness that points the way toward eternal life. That light comes from the glory realm.

Imagine that our spiritual journey begins when we board a divine passenger train on its way to the glory realm. The stories in this chapter are eternal moments that flash as vignettes through its windows. As we travel vicariously through the landscapes of Sister Ruth Carneal's testimony in these pages, we can taste and see God's goodness in the happenstances and miracles shining from within her stories.

Whether faint or beaming, the evidence of glory in our testimonies reveals God's movements. Sister Ruth is just one witness who submits to the will of the Lord. Imagine what may be accomplished if every person says "yes" to Him. His glory would extend from our private lives to the uttermost regions of the world. We could literally create Heaven on Earth. What are we waiting for? Time is short. All aboard the glory train! (*Sister Ruth now testifies of her travels around the world.*)

THE LITTLE

One day, God told me to get a dog. I really didn't want a dog. At the time, I kind of loved myself more, but God knew what I needed, so I got a dog. He was a little Shih Tzu. Most of the time, he was friendly. Do you know that I fell in love with that dog? Yes, I did. I loved him even when he didn't want to love me. I could love him because I had the love of God in me.

When he didn't like to be kissed or held, I would tell him, "That's all right. I have enough love in me for both of us." When you walk in the glory, you will have enough love in you for all of your enemies. I know that you will.

Like most people, whenever I prepared to go somewhere, I locked all of my doors. Being considerate of my dog, I would put the window down for him so he could enjoy fresh air. Then I would go out and run my errands. Sometime later, I would return home. Don't you know that my little dog would be hanging out of the opened window?

I really have to laugh at myself. What was I thinking? Anybody could have reached into the window and taken my dog. He would never run away from people. He never pulled away. He would just stand and wag his tail. He would bark, hoping that someone would come over and pet him. He was friendly to strangers. Anyone could have taken him in a moment.

A friend came to my house and asked me, "What does it mean when you see purple around a dog?" I asked her, "When did you see it?" She answered, "Just now." My friend is an intelligent woman. She wasn't imagining things.

I said, "Oh, the glory is on my dog." God put the glory upon my dog. Yes, He did. God was watching over my dog while I was gone, open window or not. The Lord puts His glory on everything. You may think that is silly, but He will put the glory, His blessings, and His presence on everything in your life.

The lesson here is to allow God to work. He will protect you and your property. He will even cause your enemies to rise up and bless you. There is great blessing in the glory realm because that is where Jesus works. The glory brings to your life deposits and strengths you didn't know exist.

You don't have to go searching, borrowing, or asking for anything in life. Just ask the Lord. He knows where everything is. He will bring it to you. What is needed will come in an overload. It will be more than you are prepared to receive. You will have so much that you will want to share what you have with others.

Sometimes what you have to share is only a bite-sized story of the foolish things you have done. That story is still a testimony of God's goodness. It contains God's power inside of it. It can touch lives to reveal God's glory working even in the little areas we often take for granted.

LOUISIANA

We aren't the only ones who can sometimes do foolish things. Our holy God does foolish things to confound the wise (1 Corinthians 1:27). You can't relate the glory to any other move of the Spirit. It's different. It is God's world that He moves in. He delights in watching us manifest how He operates. As I said earlier, it seems as if we are entertaining the Lord. He takes great pleasure in us.

By now you know that the Lord speaks revelation to me in songs. One day, a song just dropped right into my spirit. I was at my morning prayer meeting in Arizona. The season was Easter and Passover. The song was about New Orleans. When I first heard the song, I asked the Lord about it.

I said, "Are you sure? I don't really want to go to New Orleans." I didn't tell the Lord, "I'm not going." I wasn't sure if the song was for me. Typically, I would feel some kind of pull in my spirit if I was going somewhere indicated by the song. But I didn't feel any kind of pull with that song.

I never get an entire song. I only know a few words or a sentence or two. I get songs because I'm a worshiper. As I do with all songs of revelation that I get, I begin to sing the song to myself. Then I keep track of events and put two and two together.

As I sang, a couple came up to me after our meeting was over. They were holding two chocolate eggs, which they gave to me as a gift. I still didn't know who my song was meant for, but I recognized that the two little eggs were important to the song's revelation. I immediately thought, *There are two people involved.*

Two days later, Sister Kathi Zadai called me on the phone. She said, "This is Kevin's wife." At the time, the two of them were living in Seattle, Washington. Sister Kathi began to explain how she and her husband were preparing to move across country to Louisiana. Brother Kevin was still working full-time while praying eight to ten hours a day. Listen, get a record like that and you will go to the moon! God will take you anywhere.

Sister Kathi said, "Will you please pray? We are about to move and we need to know the timing." I said, "Oh, I don't have to pray, honey. I've been singing this song all day long. I know it's for you."

When she had called me, I had been thinking about the two chocolate eggs I had received. I immediately recognized, "Oh, they are the ones!" That's the glory. God will tell you things ahead of time.

I didn't know that Brother Kevin was in the same room with his wife when she called me. I had no idea what was going on, fourteen hundred miles away. As Sister Kathi and I talked, she shared the things I was saying with her husband.

Apparently Brother Kevin had some concerns. At the time, he wasn't sure if God spoke to people through songs. Now he knows differently and that my story was true. That little song prophesied what the couple were about to do. The song went like this, "They took a little bacon, and they took a little beans, and they went on down to New Orleans." That was the song!

I didn't know it then, but as I was speaking with Sister Kathi, a word of the Lord came to her husband. God told him, "Go over to that tree." They had an artificial tree in their home. It had a base that was covered with Spanish moss. The Lord then said, "Reach down in there and take out two eggs." Brother Kevin had asked, "What?" The Lord continued. "This will be a sign that she is telling you the truth."

As Sister Kathi and I were busy chatting, Brother Kevin walked over to the tree and put his hand into the Spanish moss. Guess what he found? There were two little eggs in there—of agate. They were like gemstones that had been hidden in the moss. Brother Kevin pulled them out and said, "Kathi, here is our confirmation!"

Brother Kevin kept those eggs. Actually, they were rocks shaped like eggs, but they confirmed my words. The Lord will confirm things, not only through someone else, but in other ways. God can move, speak, and do things in many ways to confirm what He is saying to us.

The Lord also led me to tell Sister Kathi, "You aren't to take much with you. You are only to take a little." Sister Kathi replied, "Oh, we are. God has impressed us to give away or sell almost everything. We are going with little." The glory was preparing to move the couple.

The key to their move was found in that little prophetic song about New Orleans. Ever since they moved, they began a journey that has led to a world-renowned ministry and school. Everything is exactly as God planned it. They only had to step out in faith.

I remember that we talked for a little while on the phone. Usually we talked about spiritual things. The answers suddenly come. Revelations surface in our conversations. In the past, when the Zadais were in town, we would spend seven or eight hours in restaurants, having tea and talking about spiritual matters. In the Spirit, I would sometimes identify and tell them things like what kinds of foods they loved, just for fun.

Now I couldn't believe everything that was coming up. God was doing and preparing to do so much! So many things were happening. They were caught up in a glory whirlwind. At one point, I remember asking Brother Kevin, "Is there room for me here?" I was wondering about all of the changes. Listen. The glory makes room for you. The glory expands and enlarges you.

I had already given Brother Kevin a prophetic word. I had told him, "You don't have a thing to worry about. You wanted to fly planes. You are going to be on airplanes. You are going to be riding with ministers. You are going to be riding on the jets. You're going to "go God." That's exactly what has happened.

The couple's move took place at lightning speed. The glory operates in a flash. When the Holy Spirit is moving, He cuts things to the chase. There wasn't a great fast or calling a lot of people to pray. It was just like "Boom!" God picked them up and flew them to the next destination in a moment. It was only a moment.

Imagine. They lived in a neighborhood that had a lot of homes that looked just like theirs. One neighbor had their home listed on the market for about a year without a sale. After Sister Kathi and I finished our phone call, the couple put their house up for sale.

Even though the Seattle real estate market was slow at the time, God sold their home in just two days! Folks in their neighborhood are still reeling about that, and the couple made an enormous profit on the sale. Do it again, Lord! That's what happens when we have a relationship with God and we say "yes" to Him.

Brother Kevin and Sister Kathi got to New Orleans. Their journey began with faith, a little song, and two good eggs. You may wonder why God didn't just give me a dream or speak to me about it. Why didn't He just say, "Kathi and Kevin are going to New Orleans"? The answer is simply that there wouldn't have been any fun in it if He had! We wouldn't have been rejoicing at all of these delicious and remarkable ways that God works.

HAWAII

Some people consider the islands of Hawaii to be an earthly paradise. When God has you traveling the world, you learn to trust in Him. Hawaii isn't exactly Eden, but God provided everything that was needed while we were in that garden. When we walk in the glory, we get a taste of what the provision of paradise is all about.

Landing in Hawaii, I had to use my last bit of money to make a phone call to our destination, a small Korean church. I called our contact's phone number. A woman answered the phone and said, "We're sorry, but the pastor isn't here any longer." Can you imagine? A traveling companion and I now had seventeen hundred dollars' worth of plane tickets to pay for so that we could fly home.

As I prepared to hang up the phone, the woman suddenly changed her tone. She said, "Wait a minute. Wait a minute. Do you pray for people?" I replied, "Oh, yes, we pray for people."

Then she asked, "Well, can you come over? We have lots of people here who need prayer."

That congregation worked us in prayer from four in the afternoon until four o'clock in the morning. We prayed all night long. And every person we prayed for put a one hundred dollar bill into an envelope for an offering.

As we were praying, the church got a phone call from another woman. Our Korean congregants had spread the word. They were calling everyone they could think of to come for prayer. I was called to the phone. A woman on the line asked, "Can you come to my house?" I said, "Well, we're over here, honey. We are praying for people here. Can you come over here?"

The woman explained her predicament. She said, "You don't understand. My husband isn't a Christian. He works at night. This is the only time that I have for someone to pray for me." She was unable to leave her home.

When we were done praying at the church, we took a cab over to the woman's house, where we prayed for her. That woman gave us five hundred dollars! Now we had all the money we needed for our plane tickets. Wasn't God wonderful? We went there on the Lord's word and He took care of us.

If you want to see Hawaii, go God's way. Do you want to go to Jerusalem? Go on the high way. Go the way where there is excitement, goodness, mercy, blessings, favor, joy, and the education of all that God is doing.

You won't come home tired. You will come home knowing more about His name and about what He loves and likes. Your real ticket to fly home on is that you will be accommodating the Lord and doing so much good for His Kingdom.

EUROPE

Years ago, a group of us were in the city of Jerusalem. The Lord impressed us to take lithographs of the city. First, we had an artist in our ministry capture the Wall and Caiaphas's house in watercolors. From those, we literally made thousands of lithographs. We had no idea what God was planning to do with them (or us, for that matter).

Suddenly, God gave someone an inheritance and the call went out, "Who wants to go to Europe?" We didn't really know what we were doing. We just heard the word "Europe." A friend had rented a villa in Europe to educate her children, so we had a place that we could all stay. A group of five of us went to Europe, simply because it was an opportunity. You have to seize opportunities when they arise.

One of the gals had lived in Israel for a long time. She said, "What shall we do, girls?" While I was trying to get my "thinker" on, she said, "How about this? Would you like to go to all of the synagogues and community centers in Europe and give each one a lithograph?"

We did. Of course, the people's favorite was the Wall, but we interchanged the pictures. It was interesting. We saw people working, but we could never find the rabbis. We didn't understand why.

We asked people, "Where are all of the rabbis?" We were told, "They have gone up to Jerusalem. It's forty years after the Holocaust. They have gone up to celebrate." We showed the people our lithographs. They asked, "Where did you find these?"

We were "on time" but we hadn't known it. It was then that we realized that we were helping the people to celebrate. We were blessing them at their triumphant moment. We were part of God's plan. Oh, it was exciting. It was really exciting!

For nearly three months, we traveled throughout Europe on beautiful trains. We had first-class tickets. We didn't mind sleeping on the trains or in depots or train stations. We only took two days off to refresh ourselves in a youth hostel.

We spent many hours worshiping. I used to just go, take another breath, and start over again. That's what you do. You breathe in and just start over. God wants to use your song. He wants to use all that He has placed inside of you.

We traveled all throughout Europe with only a light suitcase. We weren't concerned or upset about what we should have or didn't have. We ate off of the streets for six weeks. We were happy to do it. We figured out that God's table is on the streets. We had paté and juice in those nice containers. We bought crackers and a piece of fruit. God provides.

When our money ran out, my friend and I still had two more days before we were to return to the village to pick up more lithographs and begin our travels again. We had eaten almost all of our food and we were hungry. We hadn't had a good meal for a while and we were down to the last bit of food. We were saving it to last for the next two days.

At some point, a beautiful couple came aboard the train we were on and took their seats next to the window. Then they pulled out a beautiful lunch bag that was very colorful. It wasn't just a little paper bag. It was a nice bag they had bought for their picnic.

They pulled a little table out and put everything on it. There were eggs and bananas. They even had a tablecloth, cloth napkins, and salt and pepper shakers. Of course, we could smell the food. I turned my head to the right so as not to look. I didn't covet what they had.

I have to throw this next part in, for good measure. I'm sure you have heard about the lepers. Maybe I have a few spots on me. I don't know. In the Scriptures, the lepers said, "If we stay here, we are going to die" (2 Kings 7:3-20). They thought their enemy was still in the camp. They said, "If we go over there, we might die as well, but we'd better do it. It's the only opportunity we have."

The lepers knew the enemy was camping around them. They also knew it was unlawful to mix with people who were well. The lepers decided to go into the Syrian camp. To their surprise, there was no one in the tents. The spoils were left behind. Do you know that God has the spoils of your journey? He has the spoils of all of your labors.

GOD HAS YOUR SPOILS

My friend and I were kind of like the lepers. We didn't smell very good. We were wearing our wool coats. Do you know what

I mean? We were hot from running to board trains. There were odors there that weren't sweet, so the couple put their window down.

The lady was wearing a beautiful fur coat. My friend and I were cold. It was wintertime and we weren't eating very much. As the couple pulled more things out of their bag to fill their little table, I got up, walked over, and put their window up. Can you imagine? The couple then put their window right back down.

I covered myself as well as I could, but I was cold. I got up and put that window back up again. Once more, the couple put their window down. This happened four times. The couple hadn't planned to get off at the next stop, but when the train stopped, they jumped off of the train, leaving everything behind for us to eat. We were looking for food to give us strength and God provided.

I hope you get a good laugh out of that. He provides. Just know that He is your provision. God takes care of you because you are His. He is our guide. He is our joy. He is our faith, and He is bringing us into the faith.

Don't worry about what things look like or how you will get somewhere. He will provide all that you need. Your job is to be aligned with Him and to persist. Don't give up, even on the little things. God values what we do for Him.

He taught my sister this lesson. She thought she hadn't done much for the Lord when we were a family of evangelists doing tent work. At the time, she had remarried and her husband wasn't saved. She was crying. He didn't understand and she was crying. She said, "Lord, I have hardly done anything for You." But

God said to her, "My child." She was in her thirties when she said this to Him.

God gave my sister a gift to play the guitar. All of us children played instruments to help with our father's ministry. The Lord began to speak to her about her life. He said, "My child, I remember all the times you put calluses on your fingers, playing guitar, to help Me. You did it without murmuring. You were helping Me."

God is looking for us to partner with Him and to help Him. You aren't going to go anywhere under your own strength or power. Let the delight of what the Lord is doing in you come forth in your song, no matter how "little" you think your efforts are. If you are willing to serve Him in the small things, He will give you the greater. He will send you to the nations.

RUSSIA-ROMANIA-TURKEY

Around the late 1980s to early 1990s, I began to hear a Russian ballet song in the night. Because it moved inside of me like a river, I knew I was going to Russia. Churches were being established there. Young pastors, who were eighteen to twenty years of age, were in charge of many of the new churches.

When we got there, God said, "It's time the doors open." We were moving with the plan and purpose of God. He moved all throughout Russia. I traveled on the trains and got to know the people. I learned to identify with them. I would even go to look for food with everyone else as I learned about the people and purpose for being in Russia.

I shared my travels with a woman who was a nurse. I talked to her about my relationship with a doctor there. She asked me if I could help with some medication. I didn't have that kind of information. I barely knew the woman. I didn't know that we would meet again.

Russia was very cold. At one point, we were awaiting a number of visas in order to return home. For thirty days, another girl and I walked the streets, praying in the Spirit. We didn't know what we were praying. We thought we were praying just to keep ourselves warm.

After returning home, the nurse I met in Russia was waiting for me. I didn't know that important plans had already been set in motion. She summoned me to Washington, D.C. She was going to return to Russia with another nurse and ten doctors.

For twenty-four years, our group would make annual trips to Russia. We helped build a hospital, an orphanage, and we assisted the Russian and Latvian people and their doctors. People from Germany and other countries eventually became involved in the projects.

This is what God was birthing in me and my friend while we walked the cold Russian streets, praying in the Spirit. We didn't know that the little we were doing at the time would birth far greater things that God had planned for later days. While we awaited our visas in Russia, God was busy enlarging Latvia.

I had no idea that I would ever return to Russia. God called me back there during a period when many territories were separating from Russia. He told me, "Get in there quickly. I'm going to use you." God was saying, "Move quickly." He always moves quickly.

One morning, the Lord spoke to me about Turkey. His words came in a song. The river inside of me was moving again. If you allow that river to flow, you will hear answers to your questions all day long. I began to sing two lines of a song. It went, "It's Istanbul, not Constantinople. It's Istanbul, not Constantinople."[1]

I didn't know that the country's name had been changed to a Christian name, but I knew from the song that I would be heading to Turkey. Two weeks later, I was at a service and my pastor was preaching about going to the nations. He called out the names of different countries that people from our congregation were hearing in their spirit.

When the pastor said "Turkey," he stopped. Then he said, "Someone is going to Turkey." Well, I was a little shy. I thought, *No, I'm not going to admit going there.* I suddenly had fear in my heart, which I shouldn't have had.

I said in my mind, *No, I'm not going to volunteer for Turkey right now.* The pastor called it out four times! How many times do we need to hear God call? I finally raised my hand. I remember that the pastor looked at me in disbelief. He wasn't a disbelieving person. He just asked, "You're going to Turkey?"

At that moment in the middle of the service, a brother who was an insurance executive jumped up. He began to dance and sing to me. "Thou shalt go to Turkey! Thou shalt go to Turkey!" Well, how much proof do we need?

I was going to Turkey. I didn't know how I was going to go. I didn't want to go by myself. The Bible says that we are to go "two by two." What one doesn't have, the other one does. We are to help one another.

My pastor had a suggestion. He said, "We are going to take another trip to Russia. Why don't you go to Turkey from there?" His suggestion would save time and money. God wants to show you how His plans work under the economy of Heaven. I said, "Okay." Do you know what? It was exciting! I prepared and packed two different wardrobes for two different countries. It was wonderful.

Leaving Russia, my ticket was changed "accidentally on purpose." God did that. He left me sitting momentarily alone in front of the Metrople, a large hotel there. Members of my group later told me that as they left me behind, I had a sad look upon my face. Well, you have to be led by the Spirit, so sometimes things get a little uncomfortable.

All I knew was that I was boarding a plane. I couldn't speak Russian and I needed to exchange some money. I was depending upon everyone else. God gave me a little spot training. He allowed things to occur to toughen me up. God wants to make you tough so the enemy won't be rough. Allow Him to toughen you so you can fight the good fight of faith.

My ticket had the wrong date on it, so I couldn't leave. I didn't understand the exchange rate for the money. People spoke to me in Russian. I answered them in English. You may think that was a bad start. I don't think that way. God was showing me that the waters can be rough, but He will make them smooth.

On my way to Turkey, our plane made an unplanned stop in Romania. We were only told to get off of the plane. I thought,

What is happening? I didn't understand. I don't usually talk to the devil. He doesn't have my time. But as I got off the plane, I said, "Alright devil. Since you stopped this plane, wherever I put my feet when I get off, I'm possessing the land for the Lord."

It's quite a distance flying from Romania to Turkey. I remember traveling second class. I didn't know at the time that Turkey was a country with twelve million people who were largely Muslim. I only knew that the Lord said that I was going to Turkey. I had no contacts and only thirty-three dollars in my pocket!

A woman was seated beside me on the plane. We were both reading our Bibles. She suddenly turned to me and asked, "Are you going into Istanbul?" I replied, "Yes." She asked, "And who do you know there?" I said, "Well, actually, I don't have a contact."

Then she asked, "Who is picking you up at the airport?" I answered, "Well, I thought I would take a bus into the city." I didn't know that the city was twenty miles away from the airport. The woman said, "Oh honey, you need help! I'm going to help you. We have a car waiting for us." I felt as if an angel was talking to me.

As I look back, I realize that God had prepared the vacation of this woman and her husband, who was a doctor, around my need. He sent them to help me. God often has His helpers in disguise. He was sending me to Turkey to minister to the Jewish people, to bring them out. God had me chauffeur-driven into Istanbul.

I didn't have the money for the nice hotel where the couple was planning to stay. I didn't know where I would stay, so I said, "God, give me some direction." Then I asked the couple, "Is there a hotel nearby that is less expensive?"

As it turned out, the only other hotel was thirty miles away. I thought, *There goes my traveling money.* I remember paying five dollars for the taxi to take me to the hotel. By the time I paid for the hotel, I only had about six dollars left. I was supposed to be staying in Istanbul for six weeks.

The end of the story is that God connected me with the government, with the Catholic Church, with the school system, and with the Jewish people there. By the end of the trip, I had one dollar left in my pocket. That was the price of the bus fare to return to the airport. Those were the stops and starts of the Lord. I didn't know how things were going to work, but God did.

He has great plans for us. There are endless possibilities and ways that the Lord works. He will open doors and connect you to people who will help you. He will give you words to speak that you have never spoken before. There will be revelations as you move for Him. He is seated on the throne. He sees everything at the same time. He puts it all together.

God gave me six weeks in Turkey. I met the person I was supposed to meet in less than twenty-four hours! It just dropped into my spirit, the way you drop a stone into water. It just ripples in your spirit. We can easily see where our help comes from.

God wants to do things. He wants to carry you from glory to glory, from plan to plan, and from excitement to excitement. The Lord's ways are wonderful. He said He will show His goodness in the land. He truly does.

While I was in Turkey, I really wanted to visit the seven churches of Asia. That had been my prayer for years, after reading about the travels of Apostle Paul, long before Turkey and Israel were ever in the picture. I thought at the time that if I could go anywhere in the world, I would visit the seven churches of Asia.

Now that I was in Turkey, I had only a few dollars in my purse. Such a visit didn't seem at all possible. One day, a woman who was hosting my stay said that her bank had just called her because someone had deposited money into her account. She told me, "I don't really have any money, Ruth. I have to go and see what this is all about." She stepped out for a little while to go to her bank.

I had learned that my hostess friend had been to America only six weeks before I arrived in Turkey. She had just received salvation in an American church. She told me, "I got saved in some place called Mechanicsville."

When she told me the address of the church, I realized that it was located on the same street where my sister lived. My sister's street only had my sister's house, one other house, and the church where the woman was saved. Listen. God knows where you live! He knows where everyone is.

When my friend returned from the bank, she was very excited. Sure enough, there was a lot of money in her bank account. She asked me, "Where would you like to go?" So, I casually answered, "Well, the seven churches of Asia." But then she announced, "Oh, we're going to take a trip! We're going to take a trip!" I had opened my mouth. As I prepared to tell her that I was sorry, but I didn't have any money to travel, she said, "Don't worry. I've got plenty of money. They tell me there is a lot of money!"

We were going on a three-day trip. I told her I wanted to go to Ephesus, Smyrna, and the Church of Philadelphia. She wasn't familiar with why I asked for that, but she agreed. It was all new to her. I remember that we were so excited, and my prayer to visit the seven churches was finally answered!

God is working on the things you ask of Him. He is planning them. He is conditioning your heart to step into them. I could not have obtained the money I needed for that trip. My faith would not have worked that amount.

I was still a new bride in Christ at the time. I was a new person in the service of the Lord, yet God heard my call. It was part of His plan to send me into Turkey. He worked one miracle after another there. It was surprise after surprise. God kept me in Turkey with only thirty-three dollars. He can certainly do that if He wants to. He can join revelation to revelation to show you that He is faithful and perfectly able.

Many years later, I am in a church called *Church for the Nations*. Many Romanians come to our church. I shared my story about traveling and possessing the land during the stopover in Romania.

One day, a couple came up to me and said that they wanted to give me a gift that came from Romania. Remember how I put my feet down in the land? The couple gave me a little pair of glass slippers as a memorial for my impromptu stopover in Romania.

God will give you a powerful testimony and insights into His doings. There are wonderful adventures you will take and lessons you will learn. There is no way to write down all of the amazing things the Lord can do (and does). Even the Word says that if everything was printed in the Scriptures, we would all be reading until Jesus returns.

INDIA-UNITED ARAB EMIRATES

I want to show you that there are higher ways to move in the purposes of God. There are wonderful ways. Prior to the first Gulf War in Kuwait, a lady friend and I traveled to India. We had our plane tickets and we had ten dollars in our pockets. We were flying to New York and then non-stop to India.

In New York, there were four hours to wait for our connecting flight. We weren't thinking about money. We just figured that once we got to India, we would ride the train to our destination and everything would be fine. We had already fasted and prayed, but God hadn't given us any spending money.

As we waited, a man from India appeared. We recognized him because he had visited our ministry. People from around the world visited our ministry. As I shared earlier, sometimes we drove three hundred miles round-trip to take people back and forth to our services.

Well, the Queen of Sheba traveled something like fifteen hundred miles to inquire about the name of the Lord and Solomon. The Queen of Sheba nearly bankrupted her treasury. She took tons of gold with her.

When the Queen of Sheba went up, she said, "It is more than what they have told me." She was talking about the name of the Lord. She was talking about who He is and how He reaches into your life with the joy and victory of who He is. The Kingdom is more valuable than all of the gold or money in the entire world. The Kingdom of God is more than what people understand. You are always busy.

Our acquaintance from India walked up to us and asked, "Where are you ladies going?" We replied, "We're going to India." We felt comfortable talking to him because we knew him. He said, "Oh, you are? When are you leaving?" We told him that God must have sent him there to give us some money because we didn't have any. Then the man said, "Can you ladies wait until I come back? I'll be back." It took him three hours to go home and come back.

When he finally returned, he gave us more than one hundred dollars. It was a lot more money than we had. Our train ride alone would be twenty-five dollars. We couldn't have afforded it with the little money we had, before the man was sent to help us out.

When we arrived in India, God connected us to a brother who had eighty-nine churches. He allowed us to minister anywhere within a three hundred mile radius. The Lord gave me a word that the man was like Jacob. He repeatedly wept as he opened doors for us on every side.

We were in India for six weeks. Sometimes it took hours to get anywhere. We went far into the interior. Our guide said that it takes a long time to get a church going because in a way the country is very primitive.

On the way out of India, our plane stopped in Dubai. I remember getting off of the plane. It had been a long haul and I was tired. Right in the middle of the main entrance of the airport, I began weeping.

I found myself looking at what appeared to be about two blocks' worth of archives of the Arab people. There were all of these little shelves and stands that held literature about the comforts of the Arab people. When I saw those, I just began to weep, right there in the airport.

My friend had already gone downstairs. We had been way inside the interior of India. The airport had washing facilities, where we were planning to shower. My friend had gone ahead of me. I slowly made my way down to where she was. When I found her, I said, "Listen. I have this big burden. I don't know what it is. I've been weeping upstairs. I had this thought." I paused and then said, "Something is going to happen at this airport that is going to touch the world."

My friend answered, "That's strange. I have been down here dancing and praising God for the last five minutes." She was dancing all over the bathroom while I was upstairs weeping. I was encouraged by her answer. I said, "Well, whatever is going to happen, it will happen quickly and God is going to take care of it." That was my thought.

Do you know that in less than six weeks the Kuwait War began? It lasted only about two weeks before God put an end to it. At the time, I had such a burden that I was fearful of telling the authorities. I thought they might arrest me, so I didn't say anything. We didn't know it, but we were in intercession at the time. We were bringing in the answer with a dance.

You know, the church has been drinking milk. Sister Ruth Heflin taught us about the flows of God. We could come into a service and know the expected end. That's the ability to see the cream of what God is doing. If we are earnest, He will give us the cream off of the top.

God wants us to feel the need and the lack in places. He wants us to feel what He wants to do and for us to be willing to speak it out. He wants to change nations. When we are obedient, we come into a new place with God. He gives direction, provision, purpose, and joy. We see the joy of the journey.

We want to be people who are open to the flow of the Lord. Let the glory bring forth the ease of the heavens. We won't be afraid of man. We will be relaxed to the point where we will worship the Lord in Spirit and truth. We won't have a difficult time opening up to God or telling others when we have a vision. We will be obedient to the Lord.

At times, there were difficulties. The question we had to ask ourselves was whether we would give up or keep going. I have learned that it is far better to press forward. Just stick with it. Stay with it because God is teaching you. We are always learning of His divine ways.

The Bible says that He will teach us. In the last days, He will teach our children by the watercourses of the oak trees. I didn't have an understanding of that for a long time. He will teach us by the watercourses, by His ways, by the ways of God (Isaiah 44:3-4).

Many people have tasted the goodness of the Lord. They are rushing in. They are rushing in on walls. They are rushing into conferences because they have had a little taste and a little touch. They feel something money can't buy. The glory can't be taught. It gives us rest from what we have been trying to escape. The glory is the rest of the Lord. It brings rest to our spirit. The glory waters the dry regions in our life as we rest in the Lord.

AFRICA

Sometimes when I traveled, I hardly knew what I was doing, yet I accomplished what the Lord ordained for me. Because the winds were blowing at such a great speed, I was carried along. Even as I trusted in the Lord and rested in Him, many times I would say to myself, "What am I doing here?"

I was given benefits that most people never receive, simply because God makes it possible. Once when I traveled to South Africa, I was taken to a gold mine. The people showed me how gold was processed. They told me that I was the only woman who had ever been in their mine. I didn't think that was such a great thing until years later.

I thought the mine was wonderful. When you see how gold is processed, it's like salvation to glory. There are crushings, washings, beatings, and fire. Then there is the temperature of the fire that melts and forms. I saw the entire process, from the dirt of the ground all the way to the gold in brick form.

I held a gold brick in my hands. It was very heavy. They valued it at around three hundred thousand dollars. That gold is precious in man's eyes. That trip to the gold mine was part of the gold in the journey of my life.

God was showing me the preciousness of His glory. The weight of God's glory is priceless. The weight of the glory represents how much you want God and how much He wants to move in you. Make every day a journey with the Lord. He is the refiner's fire and the fuller's soap (Malachi 3:2).

When the heavy weight of the glory comes, you will fall out under the Spirit. You want this. You want to take it all in. When you get to a certain place of prayer, it seems as if God is performing an operation in you.

This is His gold. During these operations, He is making deposits in you. He wants to put you onto His operating table. He wants to remove some things and deposit some things. When God operates, He gives you a good anesthetic! You don't feel it. He does a quick work, a fast work, a perfect work.

Allow Him to do it. Let Him examine the cause in you, especially if you feel that something has stopped the flow of what He was doing. Ask Him, "Lord, I need another examination. There is something that is blocking me from hearing and receiving from You." Push the matter to the gate. Do you know the gates of hell that try to stop you? Push the battle to the gate and say, "Lord, I want to know!"

You will eventually come to a place where you feel like a pipe that the Spirit just runs through. I experienced this in South Africa. It's a place where you have no control. You're not in charge at all. You know it and it's okay.

God's Spirit is running through you and out to the people. It goes out into the room. He is anointing everything, using you as a conduit. You have become a pipeline from Heaven. You have become an open window He can look through. You are an open door He can walk through. That's the place you want to get to. You want to be used by the Lord. It's His power flowing through you.

I used to observe how some preachers were so happy. I wanted to be that happy. I was suffering for the Lord. I really was. He was trying to get "Ruth" out of the picture. He was trying to bring forth the way, the truth, and the life of what He is all about. We need to appreciate our Lord and all that He does, even when things seem difficult.

Our time with the Lord is extremely precious. We want to see revelation. But we really want revelation to the point where we see the pool of Bethesda in our daily prayer life. We want to see healings and deliverances. We want to see miracles occur even before we get there.

Many people walk at this level of glory. Reinhardt Bonnke was one such great man of God. The Lord sent me to Africa for thirty-two weeks. Over eight months, we went from Egypt all the way out to Senegal on the western side of Africa.

One morning, someone told me that we were going to see Reinhardt Bonnke. I was still half asleep while they dressed me and took me over to his ministry. Seeing him was like a prize. He gave me a whole day of his time. When I arrived, I began speaking about the living creatures, not knowing that his plan was to preach on that topic in just three days' time. He was going to a big groundbreaking ceremony for Ray McCauley.

A Rainbow ministry colleague at the time had about twenty-seven thousand people in his church. He stopped everything and gave me an apartment and a chauffeur-driven car. I even had a washing machine. You know, women want such things. I didn't know that Johannesburg, South Africa is a very modern place.

A revival was running in full pledge, at full speed. We were there at the right time. God has perfect timing. I met every spiritual leader and presidents and vice-presidents. I met governmental leaders. God gave me words for them and they gave me favor. I had so much favor. I couldn't believe how much favor there was! I couldn't handle it all.

I went to one church in South Africa where the water of the Spirit was waist-deep in front of me. I kept trying to get around it, but I couldn't. I tried to step into it, but I thought, *I'll drown.* There was such a presence of the Lord there!

We went into a prayer room. The walls were padded. I had never experienced this level, this depth of the presence of the Lord. The Lord said to me, "This is the way it was on the day of Pentecost." It wasn't me operating in there. It was the Spirit. The Spirit just flowed.

That night we had such a depth of the presence of the Lord that it looked like a whirlpool. I was trying to get around it. I thought, *I can't. I have to go through it. I have to step into it.* We have to step into this new place. It's a holy place. It's the place where angels are ministering. That night, I only prayed for one person, but I felt as if I had prayed for everyone.

There may have been a fire in that room. I'm serious! I laid my hands on one man. Holy fire burned all the way through his body. The carpet was the color of his shoe soles. The fire burned the imprint of his soles into the carpet! We tried to capture it on film with ten different cameras, but couldn't. Maybe God didn't want it taken out of there. It was meant just for that place.

We were going one way and the pastor said, "Let's go another way." It was the way of the Lord. We prayed all afternoon to know the mind of the Lord in that place that was so heavily endowed with the Spirit of God.

I returned the next day before the service began. Someone was kneeling on the floor, trying to scrub something up with soap and water. I said, "What's this?" They said, "Oh, someone tracked in something from outside." I said, "No, that wasn't it." The power of the Holy Spirit had burned a quarter-inch deep mark into the carpet. The glory was like a lightning force.

The Lord has a branding iron in His hand. He is branding people with His name. He is putting His name, His identity, and His desire upon us. He is marking His people who know their God and who shall do exploits.

You know, you can tell when your water level is low. You can even discern the level of faith that is in a church when you enter. You can tell if there is any faith at all. I'm not telling you to leave your church, but check the level. Join a church that has the same vision that God has placed in your heart.

We want this level of power. We want His power to fully operate in us. We want His charge inside of us. Wherever we go, things should change. Atmospheres should change. People should change. At that level, the favor of God comes upon you. You have built a holy place for the Lord to do His work. He can do what He wants in you. It's as if your holy temple has His altar fire burning within it.

The power disappeared from the South African church after only two years. The Spirit of revival left that place. It just faded.

The glory will leave us if we don't remain diligent in prayer. The Bible says, "Pray without ceasing" (1 Thessalonians 5:17 KJV). Always call upon the Lord. Always be in prayer and seek His face. His glory will come and remain for as long as people are diligently seeking Him.

It has never been hard for me to pray long hours. During my time in Africa, the Lord said, "I want you to pray eight hours a day for twenty-five days." You know, after two hours of prayer, I ran out of words, so I prayed in tongues. I took someone with me. When I got sleepy, she prayed in tongues and that would awaken me.

The head of a big city in a country next to Ethiopia spoke to me one day while I was preaching. I happened to mention Sister Heflin to him. He stopped the entire meeting just to ask me about her. He said, "Did you say Ruth Heflin?" I said, "Yes. She's my friend." Then he said, "Do you know that woman came to our country and turned it upside down?" Some government officials had asked Sister Ruth Heflin for direction, wisdom, and advice.

When the man asked me if I knew Sister Heflin, right away I thought, *Oh, brother.* I used to beg God to give me mercy, but He didn't listen. He never gave me a dream. I just asked Him for His highest gift. His answer to me was to send Sister Ruth into my life. He had her train me because my calling was to the nations.

The Lord never told me, "I'm going to send you to Africa." No. Our congregation "prayed in" one hundred thousand dollars. Someone from the Coca-Cola Company came to our ministry. They donated one hundred thousand dollars. We were in prayer when they said, "Send your people who want to travel, anywhere they want to go." There were about twenty people in all.

Another time, a girl came to our ministry camp. She said, "I know you have someone in this camp who wants to go to Africa. If you will tell me who it is, I will pay all of their expenses. I'll buy the tickets. I'll get all of the visas." That is exactly what happened.

Before I ever went to Africa, I went into a prayer room to seek the face of the Lord. It wouldn't be a light thing that the Lord would do. It would be a great thing. I remember that I had looked at a world map. As I listened for the voice of the Lord, I heard, "Thirty-two weeks."

I was looking on the map at the continent of Africa, when the Lord spoke. I didn't know that I would be traveling to Africa. Somebody else, who was from another state, also heard the word, "Africa." They came running.

We should always wait for a word from the Lord before we travel or serve Him. We all need to wait on the Lord. Have someone pray over you. Hear from God. You need to hear that you are coming back. You need to hear about the things that will happen, even before you go.

The Lord had said to me, "Prepare yourself, My daughter, for you are going to be gone away from home a long time. There are many things I want to show you, many places and many people I want you to meet. I will cause you to meet all the spiritual leaders of every country that you go to in Africa, if you will prepare yourself."

I knew what the Lord meant. It meant fasting, praying, and reading the Word. I had three months to prepare. God put me on a fast. I will guarantee that it was more than forty days long. He said "no food." It's a little water and then you get to that place. It's a supernatural thing.

It was very different traveling with the African people because of the journey, the activity, and the many places I went to among the natives. We went to the Maasai tribes. We would enter a lot of enemy territory as we ministered four times a day. We had come into a place with God that required a lot of fasting and prayer. We were praying eight hours a day.

Was it easy? No. But after a few hours, you pray in tongues. You take a breath and keep drinking water and swimming in the river. You just keep getting more of God. Everything we did took place from a place of prayer.

You don't have to seek money. You are to seek the wisdom of God and what He is doing. Get understanding and the knowledge of what God is doing. I am talking about a *walk*. You will be like Enoch. You will step into the heavens and you won't come back.

You will have constant conversations with the Lord that come out of your heart. You will constantly think about Him and ask Him questions. You are serious about Him. Your labor will not be in vain. God will work so quickly. You may feel at times that it's hard to keep up with Him.

Let your home and your table where you eat be a round table of the Lord. I never eat unless I am thankful to God for what He has given me. I am thankful for everything. I rejoice over it. I take nothing for granted.

We are called to be a voice for the Lord for our nations. Let your voice be heard in the heavens! Cry aloud unto the Lord and spare not. Let your voice be heard. Let it take charge. Let it take hold of the wishes of the Lord. You will see God turn things around.

I had a vision of a great ship in the water. A ship moves by one little finger on its rudder. That tiny rudder turns that big vessel. I saw that the countries of the world are like a big ship. I saw that ship come up out of the water. The whole front end came up out of the water. I saw God turn that ship around.

God wants to take us where no big ministry ship or even a tiny ministry boat with oars has ever been (Isaiah 33:21). If He has to change the world using one person, He will do it. He desires that we all flow and go together. We are to synchronize ourselves. He desires unity. He wants to unite the nations with His glory.

AUSTRALIA

I mentioned earlier that God sometimes calls us to minister in a moment. Years ago, I was in Australia ministering and preparing to return home. I already had my plane ticket ready. I was planning to leave in the morning. I have found that when you have a little leftover time, people will ask you to squeeze in another service. Many times I have run from the airport to do a last-minute service.

It was late in the evening when someone heard about Sister Ruth Heflin. A friend of mine was talking to a man about me. She apparently told him, "This sister has a few hours. Would you like her to come?" Before I knew it, I was volunteered to go somewhere. The man accepted me on the merit of my relationship with Sister Heflin. He said, "Any friend of hers would be good."

You really want to have a service where you don't have to be concerned about what you are going to appreciate or preach. The Spirit of God just falls and does all that He needs to do. You need to know how to align yourself so that what God wants to happen can happen.

At the service, I went into the bathroom to look for a word from the Lord. I was waiting and asking, but nothing was happening. It was so quiet that I heard someone in the other room ask, "Where is Sister Ruth?" There is something about the water in a bathroom. It cleanses you. It washes you. Many people have said that there is something about running water that moves the heart of God to speak.

I went to the service and we began to sing. When worship began, that was the end of "Ruth" and the beginning of Jesus. Nearly everyone, including the pastor, was slain on the floor by the Holy Spirit. For a moment, I didn't realize what had happened. My eyes were closed as I sang. I didn't hear any other voice but my own. When I opened my eyes, the musician and I were the only two people in the room who were still standing.

There are levels of the presence of God that will come. You remain standing if He has charged you to that level. You can stand the greater heights of His glory. We want to flow in the Spirit and not from what we have learned or what someone else has said.

The Bible says there is a single interpretation of the Word (2 Peter 1:20). We have to be speaking from the glory realm when we preach. That's where the glory, the power of God is. He is the one who gives us His interpretation of His Word. Sometimes things don't go quite the way we think they should go. Things just happen. You wonder if you heard the voice of the Lord correctly.

On another trip to Australia, I was supposed to turn to the right, but I turned to the left. God always wants us to turn to the right. I had a day when I wasn't working. The people around us wanted to use us that day. I had paid my way and had a little say-so. I chose to obey man instead of God. That will wear you out! I went in the wrong direction.

I know now that when God uses you, He has a schedule for you. He wants us to be as direct and apt as we can be. We are to move with that glory cloud. Always move with friends who are in the cloud. Amen?

I was ministering in New South Wales. Everything was prepared for us. A man gave us automobiles and a building. He emptied out a hotel and paid for all of the rooms so we could have total occupancy in the hotel. He even brought in cooks to cook for us. It was a beautiful building, decorated in pink and mauve. It was a glorious old theater that was converted into a house of God. Everything looked good. Everything was ready for me.

I should not have gone there. At one point, I backed up too far. I hit a monitor and broke my arm in two places. The pastor, who had allowed me to use the building, also had an accident. He backed up into the other monitor. I didn't know it at the time, but he broke two ribs.

I will be careful here with my words. At one point, I wondered if God was maybe telling the pastor not to have the meeting. We are to walk carefully, circumspectly. We are to walk following the ways of the Lord.

I still had a two-week revival in Tasmania. I had to go to the revival. There were many hard moments on that trip. I'm a woman who was self-employed. I liked to take care of myself. I liked doing things my way.

God was breaking down all of those walls through those events. Maybe He allowed it or it was going to happen. I don't think that the Lord said, "I'm going to crush her." I'm not saying that. I stepped back too far. When I hit that monitor, I thought it cut right through my body. I thought I was cut in two and I was about to die.

For twenty-four hours, I laid with my hands across my chest. I couldn't move anything. It was painful just to move my little finger. I don't know all that God was doing in that pain. I do know that He was speaking to my heart about some things.

I still preached at the revival. Every morning someone had to dress me. That was hard because of my independence. It was very difficult. You have to unwrap everything and just give it all to God. You have to say, "Here it is. I'm not holding it for myself anymore. I want You to do what You want to do, need to do, and must do in my life." Amen? You can say "Amen." That's about the only real choice we have. Say "Yes" and "Amen" to the Lord. Allow Him to do what He wants to do in you. We used to sing those words in a song.

Despite the pain, for two weeks at that revival we sat in the glory. For fourteen days and for two services a day, we sat in that glory. For at least three of those days, in the morning, no one could even speak. We would just start laughing and falling under the power of God.

It got to the point where three hundred people didn't speak when they went out or came into the meetings. They felt such an awe of the Lord. When people left, they wouldn't say a word. You didn't know they were leaving. It was like looking at the passion of Christ. It was that kind of an atmosphere. The glory returned for two weeks. It was like rain in our eyes. We could hardly see.

The glory of the Lord appeared like smoke. It would hover over people. We would lie down until God gave us enough consciousness to get up and go home. The power got into my legs to the point where I could barely walk. People had to pick me up and carry me home.

My joints actually ached. God was firing our bones. The fire actually gets into your bones. They hurt a little bit. I have to almost be carried. It is like Jell-O. You can't walk. But you have to get back into the glory. You see, God was charging my body.

He wants to do that to you, too. It was an awesome time! Oh, we were so happy! Praise God. He works all things out for the good of all who love Him (Romans 8:28). We need the rain of His glory. We need revival in our churches because people everywhere are so thirsty.

THE PHILIPPINES

Many times during our travels, things seemed impossible. There was never any money to begin with, yet God would always provide. When Sister Heflin and I went to the Philippines, one of our opportunities allowed us to drop flyers from an airplane. How we ever rented that airplane, I really don't know. We dropped all of those little printed flyers over the city of Manila. I don't know where the money came from. It cost a little money.

But you see, Sister Heflin was a woman with a vision to go into the whole world. So when she asked me to go with her, I knew that I had to lay my life on the line. I just knew that. Now that I think about it, Sister Ruth wasn't a hard person or difficult. I don't remember having arguments or misunderstandings about anything. There were difficulties and persecutions enough in the world.

When Elisha followed Elijah, he had to return to the crossing of the Jordan. Great things happened there. It wasn't a river that would sustain a boat, but it was the crossing-over point for the Israelites. It was where Joshua and the priests crossed over into the new.

I knew there would never be the kinds of opportunities anywhere else for me that Sister Ruth could provide. In our church, we had to pass inspection. That's not how God operates. He is looking for a willing heart. We simply need to be willing to go. Any difficulties we encounter are part of learning how to come into the greater things. Eat the bitter with the sweet and give portions to those who are weak.

I once took a pastor's underage daughter to the Philippines. I didn't have the right papers. I didn't even think about papers. I could have said by the Spirit that she was my granddaughter and gotten away with it. You can make up or create something, but God doesn't want you to add to or take away. He wants what we do to remain pure. Let it be very pure and of a pure strength.

If you want to travel, then get yourself a passport and keep it up to date at all times. You are going to need it. Those officials took the little girl's passport because we didn't have everything in order.

The next day, we had to travel for miles to retrieve her passport. We exchanged transportation three or four times in an all-day trip just to get there. I thought, *We won't get back until late at night. Lord, help us.*

I kept asking God for a sure word. "Give me a word. Give me it, Lord. Let it be that they will hear." You know, the Philippines were really the only Christian nation between the United States and Jerusalem at that time. The Charismatic Movement had come into the Catholic Church.

I just told the little girl, "Let's go, honey." When we got to the government office to get her passport, there was a roomful of people. God gave me a sure word that day. Those people love their religion or even the Charismatic Movement. The whole Philippine Islands were like that.

When it was our turn, the official said, "And what are you here for?" Listen, you only have a moment. *Buy the moment.* I said, "Sir, we have come to bless your country. We forgot to get the necessary papers for our little friend here. The pastor said that he wanted her to come here to learn more." The official didn't even let me finish. He turned to his workers and said, "Give the lady what she wants."

God said, "I work in a moment. I'll tear down. I'll root up. I'll plant in a moment what you need." God is in a hurry. He also said, "I will cause your descendants" (Isaiah 54:3). "I will make the desolate cities full of Myself. I will make them inhabited." Do you want to inhabit? Do you want to be taken over for God, or merely take over? Which do you want?

This isn't a makeover. It isn't a movie. This isn't just a moment. This is *eternity* that we are talking about. It's knowing God and what He wants. I always ask the Lord "God, give me the secret. Give me the revelation."

When you worship God, you get prophetic words. You don't just speak or sing because you have a nice voice. There are a lot of songbirds out there. God has taught me to listen for the prophetic word. When you hear it, you speak it if He moves you to do that. His words will open doors all over the world.

Cayman Islands

I never had a birthday party until I was forty-three years old. We didn't get cake and all of the things that other people normally get. My mother would give us a blessing on our birthday. People spend so much money on frills. Don't waste your time or your money. Save it. There are poor people all over the world who can live off of your birthday for a year! Take what you wanted to consume for a moment and let it last for a year on someone else.

People say that God has plenty of money. That is true and we are to be servants of it. We are His servants. We have to handle the birthday party first if we are going to handle a nation. Whatever God gives you, do it with excellence.

One year, Sister Heflin wanted to send me to the Cayman Islands for my birthday. I didn't know it at the time, but it is very expensive to go there. I also didn't know what kinds of things were going on down there at the time.

I wanted a certain position given to me because it was an opportunity that few people get to have. Sister Ruth came and asked me if I would be willing to give the position up for someone else. What did I say? "Oh, sure." Sister Ruth was the head there. She knew what was going on. She also knew I didn't want to give up that position. But I said, "Okay." I surrendered myself to the process.

Later on, she asked if I would like to go to the Cayman Islands for my birthday. I thought, *Who is paying for this?* I didn't really want to go. It wasn't because of the expense. I really wasn't interested in going there. I wanted to go for a ministry purpose, not for myself. Sister Ruth sent me to the Cayman Islands to Brother Benny Hinn's crusade that was there. To this day, I don't know how that trip happened so quickly. Sister Ruth and I just went there.

At the event, Sister Ruth said, "Go up and introduce yourself to one of the staff members." I said, "Sister Ruth, I'm not good at that. I'll probably fumble all over myself." I was saying, "Don't make me do this. Please don't make me do this." But she said, "No, you just go."

On the way there, I realized that I had left my billfold with all of my money in the bathroom. I hoped that no one would come into the bathroom and take it. That was the first thing that happened to me. I left my money in the bathroom. I did get it back, but I felt that it was going to be one thing after another.

God wanted me to speak to a specific person, so He brought her right to me. She just appeared in front of me even before I could introduce myself and say that I knew Sister Ruth. I knew that a person's name can sometimes bring you favor. The Lord wants *His* name to bring you favor. It's His name. His name is everlasting.

As I prepared to introduce myself, I heard the words, "She's a thoroughbred." So, I said to the woman, "Do you know what? I'm a friend of Ruth Heflin. The Lord said to tell you that you're a racehorse. You're a thoroughbred." The woman exploded. She was from Lexington, Kentucky, where there are a lot of horse farms. People raise race horses from all over the world there. It's a good place to be from.

I had some minor concerns about mixing with Benny Hinn's group. The woman said, "You're not staying out here with everyone else. You're coming with us to help us pray for people." She said this to me just on that one word of knowledge I gave to her.

I did meet Pastor Benny Hinn. He was very careful about people who sat around him. He said to me, "Sister, do I know you from somewhere?" My back was facing him when he said this. I turned and said, "Well, Ruth Heflin is my friend." Sister Ruth had given Pastor Hinn a prophetic word before he ever entered the ministry. She told him that he was going to be a world-renowned minister.

God set all of this up for me because I was willing to give up a position that I had really wanted. He gave me the biggest birthday party I had ever seen. There was food and music. It was wonderful. It was beyond my imagination. It was more than I could handle. I really didn't know what to do with myself!

I don't know if I was ready for it, but it was one of those favors that the Lord will give to you. Sometimes we aren't ready for it. When you are faithful and you go after the Lord, He favors you. You want to move to those higher levels. You will get there if you are willing to sacrifice a little to move in the glory with Him.

DOMINICAN REPUBLIC

When you work for the Lord, you become His ambassador. Earthly ambassadors will send for you to come and help them. That happened to me in the Dominican Republic. I met with a mother who had several children. She asked, "Will you pray for my children?" I chose only to pray for one of her children, a young man. I had a vision that the boy would be in an accident.

That day, an accident paralyzed the young man from the neck down. I was preparing to return home when the family called me on the phone and asked, "Will you pray?" I felt all of this joy. I said, "It's okay. He is going to be healed!" I knew it. I just knew it by all that God presented to me.

Three months after I returned home, the family called me again. I told them to put the phone to the young man's ear. I said to the Lord, "Lord, what is the key to this man coming alive?"

He showed it to me. The young man was embarrassed about his situation. He couldn't talk. He could hardly groan. So, I said, "Lord, take away the embarrassment." All of a sudden, I heard yelling through the phone. The young man hadn't spoken for three months.

The ambassador to the Dominican Republic heard about the miracle and called me from Washington, D.C. I didn't know who he was, so he had to tell me. He asked, "Can you come to visit me?" I said, "What do you need?" It was Passover. He said, "I want the Holy Ghost."

I drove to Washington, which was difficult. I don't know my way around some of these places. I stepped over the threshold of the man's house and God stepped into his life. We want God's presence, His glory upon us.

From across the room, the man began to speak in tongues. His wife started weeping, which was difficult for her. She just wept. God's glory and power should be so strong around you that He takes everyone by surprise and transforms people without you having to say a single word.

THE GREAT

We hear many things in the news. Do we ever think about what lies behind the stories we hear? Decades ago, *Time* magazine had a story of the day and a story of the hour. That may be exciting or stirring, but it's not your flesh that needs to be stirred. We should stir the Spirit. Stir it. Shake yourself. Shake off the old. God is doing things in a new way. Your speech, your vocabulary, and your understanding are going to change under the glory.

While we were still in Jerusalem and serving in Sister Heflin's ministry there, a group of us received a prophetic word. One day in high worship, someone began to prophesy. The Word of the Lord was, "You will hear terrible news that will happen in the Canary Islands. Look not at the scenes and the tragedy but to Me. For through it, not because of it, *I will answer a mother's prayer.*" God was only speaking about one person.

We heard that word. We distinctly heard the Lord say, "I will answer a mother's prayer." We didn't exactly know what that meant. I don't remember a lot of the rest of the prophecy, but I remember that part.

Sometime later, two of our friends who had been in our meeting on the day of the prophecy were now in California. They had attended a meeting where a man gave his testimony about an airline tragedy in the Canary Islands. The man had been a passenger on one of two airplanes that were involved in a crash that day.[2]

The witness shared that he always told his mother goodbye before he went on a trip. One of his associates and the associate's wife were supposed to go with him that day. For some reason, the wife couldn't go. So the man and his associate boarded the plane without her. Mid-flight, something happened and their plane was forced to land at the Canary Islands for maintenance and to refuel.

As they waited on the ground, another plane was also diverted. That plane landed so close to the man and his associate's parked plane that the passengers on both aircraft could see one another's faces through the windows. In that moment, they didn't know they were looking at eternity.

Some time went by and both planes were on the tarmac preparing to take off. There was fog and confusion that day. The plane that took off first lost sight of the plane with the man and his associate. The plane that was taking off ran into the other plane, instantly igniting both aircraft. In a moment, nearly six hundred souls aboard the two planes were taken away.

The witness testifying was one of only a handful of survivors. He said that at the time of impact, he could hear Scriptures spoken that he had never heard before. Angels began reciting Scriptures over him. They seemed to come from every direction.

The man didn't exactly know how he got out of his seat. He just remembered that his partner was missing. Both planes were burning. He heard God speaking over him every second he was on the plane.

He described how, at some point, he was ejected out of his seat to find that he was standing on the airplane's wing. Scriptures were still coming to him as he jumped off of the wing onto the tarmac. The Lord continued speaking to him throughout the ordeal.

The man who shared his testimony said that he had become very discouraged after all that had occurred. His mother had shared some things with him that God had told her the morning they prayed before the man went on his trip. When he left the house that day, his mother had wept over him. They didn't know what was happening at the time, but intercession had taken over their lives.

Amazingly, the man wasn't burned, but he broke his leg. He was the only survivor who wasn't burned. He was also the main character retelling the horrific story in *Time* magazine. His face appeared on the front cover. The man's associate also survived the crash, but he was burned and had to leave the business.

At some point in his life, the man had asked God to make him a minister, a preacher of the Word. However, he had gone into business instead of following his calling. As the man gave his testimony at the California meeting, he revealed his discouragement. He wasn't seeing great results. He didn't understand that it's here a little and there a little.

A friend of ours who attended the meeting where the man testified had shouted, "Brother! Brother! Don't be discouraged!" Those words encouraged the man to such a degree that a new mantle was placed upon him and he picked up his faith. Now he had a suitcase full of faith. It wasn't just full of ideas. He took off running for the Lord!

He wasn't a young man, either. I declare that he was about sixty or sixty-two years old. He ended up coming to our ministry camp in Ashland, Virginia to share what the Lord had done for him.

Do you remember what the Lord told us in Jerusalem? He said, "I will answer a mother's prayer." We were on Mount Zion when God spoke to us about the accident, just a few months before it took place. We heard what Jesus had to say about things before the accident even happened.

Sometimes we want God to know all the details of what we have been through. We forget that He already knows it all! He knows that some of us haven't really suffered that much. We will all suffer in some way. You can't know the Lord without appreciating how He suffered for you. I'm not talking about doing without or not having what you want.

I am talking about how the waiting is sometimes unbearable. When a mother is getting ready to bring forth a child, she wants it to happen right now because of the birth pains. There are birth pains in the Earth today. Part of those pains is the strain of waiting for the new things to come forth. We spend a lot of time waiting on the Lord.

We have to be patxient and persistent in our faith walk. The glory will come in. Just be diligent and listen for God's voice. He wants you to hear what He has to say about you. Remember that God can do anything! I don't care about impossibilities. God doesn't even look at them.

ALL THINGS ARE POSSIBLE WITH GOD

He says that He knows the number of hairs on your head. Saints, He isn't just talking about how He has them all counted. He is saying that He knows all we aren't aware of and all we can't see. Whether there are little foxes or big giants, it really doesn't matter. He knows everything. He wants you to be aware that He is on the throne. If He has to, He will rise up, just like He did for Stephen (Acts 7:56).

God would rather that we come up to where He is. He says, "Come up higher" (Luke 14:10). God wants us to go higher and higher, into the clouds. He says, "My ways are in the clouds. They are hidden. They are in the secret place." That's where He wants them. You know, God can keep secrets better than we can!

He wants you to find them and to discover how precious, wonderful, and costly they are. We put a high value on anything precious. We put a lot of insurance on it. You have the best insurance you can get when you have the assurance that Jesus is your Lord.

HOMELAND

Jerusalem is a place of change as much as it is a place of identity and direction. Israel is the plumb line of the Earth. God is checking all of the nations around Israel to see how they are treating her. God said that Jerusalem would be "a praise" in all the Earth.

I can tell you stories about the blessings that have come to those who partner with Israel. I can also tell you stories about some of the judgments that have come when people try to give Israel's land away or try to make her do something that God hasn't ordained.

When you go to Israel, things happen. I feel at home there. I have found my resting place. There is a darkness that disappears. Light seems to shine forever in what God is doing there.

Scripture says, "On the side of the north, give her no rest until she is made a praise in all the Earth" (Isaiah 62:7). Most of the priests of the rabbinical order live in Jerusalem. Mount Zion is truly the oasis of the world. It's the homeland of God's chosen people.

One evening, I was coming home from church. It was just before Passover. In the back roads of my mind, I heard a song.

The words wouldn't come in, so I began to hum. The song still wouldn't come together. I heard only a little here and there.

All of a sudden, "Boom." The song broke open inside of me. It was the song *Exodus*. I knew that I was going to Israel. In a day or two, I got a phone call. Someone from another county was calling for prayer. A situation had occurred and a man needed someone to pray.

I said to him, "No, we aren't going to pray. We are going to declare that God will resolve this whole situation in a moment." Don't talk about the problem. Talk to God and watch Him bring deliverance.

When we were about to hang up, the man said, "Oh, by the way, we're going to Israel. Would you like to go?" I simply replied, "Sure." It just popped out! Then I asked rather boldly, "I have a friend that would like to go, too." Can you imagine? The man replied, "Oh, we'll pay for that too." They paid for both of us!

On another occasion, Sister Cindy Jacobs was ministering over at CBN.[3] A group of us including me and Sister Ruth Heflin were invited to attend the event. We were given a nice table. I am sorry to say that I was just a little uninterested that morning. That really wasn't nice and I have cried a lot over that moment. I excused myself to go to the restroom to get my spirit straightened out. I went there for an adjustment. Everything was coming out of me in the wrong way.

While I was gone, Sister Cindy came over to our table. It was the only table in a room of about four hundred people that she chose to minister to. When I returned, I was told, "You missed it!" I asked, "What did I miss?" My friends told me, "Sister Jacobs ministered to everyone!"

I was so sorry. I built an altar of tears over that. I felt horrible. I didn't know that we would have a private audience with Sister Cindy later on. We would meet up with her in her hotel room. When we got there, I waited for a quiet moment when Sister Cindy and I were the only ones in the room.

As she busied herself searching for something in her purse, I began to explain to her how I had missed her stop at our table. I told her that I was so sorry. I don't beg for words, but I asked, "Do you have a little left so you can give me something?" Sister Cindy didn't even turn toward me as she said, "Well, as a matter of fact, I do."

Her purse had a long strap. I watched her pull her fingers across that strap as if she was measuring out a word for me. She said, "You're going to have to go suddenly. It's going to be out of your schedule and out of your timing. You're going to have to go suddenly. You're going to take a trip to Israel."

One morning, not long after the prophecy, I was in Sister Ruth Heflin's abode, watching her from a window on the second floor. Earlier in the day, she looked at me and said, "I'm not going round in circles. I'm going around. I'm walking around Jesus right now."

But later on as I watched from an upper room, Sister Ruth was now outside and walking back and forth on the sidewalk. She looked like she needed something, so I opened the window and asked, "Is there something you need?" She looked up and said, "I need somebody to go to Jerusalem. Do you want to go?" There was the "suddenly" from Sister Cindy's prophecy, right there.

So, I asked her, "When?" and she replied, "Right now." I was already dressed. Get dressed in the Spirit and be prepared. I added, "But I don't have anything packed!" Undeterred, she announced, "I've already sent two people." Those two people came up to my room and packed my suitcase for me. I went downstairs and we were gone in ten minutes.

The Lord was sending me to Israel on an assignment. He even delayed the airplane so that we could be on it. Imagine. It was a one hundred and ten mile drive to get to the airport in Washington, D.C.

At one point when we were in Jerusalem, Sister Ruth asked me, "How would you like to go around the world?" I thought about it. She encouraged my answer with, "Will you say yes?" How many of us are ready to say "yes"? The bride always says "yes." We are always at the altar of God. We are to obey Him and to be fully surrendered unto Him.

I can share some of these stories now because with things that are hidden in the glory, it's all about the timing. My assignment at the time was to bring back personal items that belonged to an adviser to the prime minister. I had to get all of his property through customs. Names were on all of the books and papers. I would have to explain them through every checkpoint. It could be tricky.

My prayer was, "Lord, don't let them open a suitcase. Don't let them open a book. Just open Yourself, Lord, as we stand there." By God's grace, that's what happened. God gives you these assignments when you allow Him to be seen. He will give you the greater things.

We are His errand persons. Wouldn't you love to know that you are a person who is on an errand for God? This is how I learned about God. I didn't really want to be in the middle of anything. I wasn't looking for anyone's anointing. I wasn't looking for anything except to please God. You know how it is. Give me my little corner.

We can't remain hidden in the world when we move with God. The only place we can hide is in His secret place. For everything else, we are to be that candle on a hill. We are to be a light unto the nations.

I recently took another trip to Israel. Somebody just called me up one day and invited me. They said, "Would you like to go to Israel?" We ended up in Israel, just like that. It just happened.

Some friends who were hosting us there were talking about a big tour that was in town. They asked me, "Have you ever heard of Sid Roth?" I said "Yes." Then they said, "Well, we're following him into Tiberius." The group wound up in Jerusalem.

I got another telephone call. Someone asked me, "Can you come over to the hotel?" It happened in a moment, in a split second. God said, "I can root. I can pluck up. I can plant. I can bring order to it" (Psalm 52:5).

I met Brother Kevin Zadai up in Israel. That's where the idea for this book came about. We had been trying different ways to do a book. A friend of mine and I spent hours on topics, but nothing clicked. I didn't feel a release. The timing wasn't there. We didn't know what God was planning. He operates in His timing. Let Him work it out.

We are in the last seconds of the time clock of God. We are in the last moments of moving for Him. Listen to the Spirit. Listen to the voice of the Lord. In the morning, He will awaken you with songs. At night, you will go to bed with a song over you.

I do know that when you come to God and you move in His realm, the glory is everywhere. It's always moving. The movements of God are in a higher realm. He wants us to come into His realm. In that realm, He will multiply. He will produce. Be ready at all times. If you are going to move in the glory, then be ready. Be minutemen and women.

NOTES

1. "Istanbul (Not Constantinople)" was a 1953 novelty song sung by the Four Lads (Nat Simon, music, Jimmy Kennedy, lyrics). The song was written to commemorate the five-hundredth anniversary of the fall of Constantinople to the Ottoman Empire.

2. History.com Editors, "Jumbo jets collide at Canary Islands airport," History, November 13, 2009, https://www.history.com/this-day-in-history/jumbo-jets-collide-at-canary-islands-airport.

3. CBN stands for Christian Broadcasting Network, an American evangelical network founded by televangelist Pat Robertson. Its headquarters are located in Virginia Beach, Virginia.

Six

ETERNAL GLORY

Lord, we declare that Your Spirit, Your waters, like a mighty sea, will begin to roll over the nations. Lord, there will be a baptism of truth that we have never experienced before. Lord, we declare that we will seek Your face and know the higher place to stand and to move in.

Just light the fire, Lord. Light the candle. Make it a new day upon us. We have never experienced, seen, or heard what You want to do, but You are going to do it because we are seeking You and because You love us and have need of us. We thank You for it, in Jesus' name. Amen.

—SISTER RUTH CARNEAL

GLORY PROPHESIES

Kevin here, friends. God is trying to reveal things to His people in a clearer way than ever before. We have matured as a body. We are beginning to seek the Lord with a greater zeal and passion. God is clarifying things for us as we open our hearts to receive all He desires to do. Let's listen in as Sister Ruth talks to us about prophesying and the glory.

(*Sister Ruth's story continues.*) The pastor of our church used to check us to see where our "water" level was. He would teach us how to prophesy and flow in the Spirit. If we didn't understand, he would teach us again. He didn't make us prophesy, but there was prophecy in every service, or else.

When we entered our prayer room before a meeting, we gathered knowing that we were going to hear from God. When we worshiped the Lord, the glory would come in and bring prophecy. We would hear from Heaven. I'm not just talking about the weather. I'm talking about hearing headlines of things that were going on in the world. We would get warnings and introductions to what God wanted to do in a new place and in a new way.

You always want to speak in the prophetic realm. You want to speak things that are happening and that are about to happen. We want to live in that realm. Prophecy clarifies. It shines the light upon areas we have never seen before. It opens an understanding that we haven't been able to know or walk in before.

Jesus said, "From this day you are going to see the angels ascending and descending" (John 1:51). We talk about the ups and downs of life, but that's not it. The Lord is showing us the ease of His glory. The glory brings forth ease. When things in the world are upside down, you will be right side up. You will say and see that God is in the middle of it.

We recently experienced turmoil in the world. People scrambled around because of a virus. The glory brings forth a rest and a knowing, even in such situations. These aren't things that I recognized right away. I guess my spirit just wasn't open. God will take us over hurdles and extremes to break us open. He wants to break off the yoke that is upon us. Don't worry. Something good will come out of it.

People didn't expect Jesus to come out of Nazareth. Something good and wonderful is coming out of this turmoil that we have been in. There will be an increase of the Lord in the wages. I'm talking about the finances of the Lord. It's the set time for increase.

Esther was there to save a nation. God is going to use us as a company of people. Great is the company to save the nations. We will have the nations in our heart and in our mouth as we declare His glory.

I'm not really a church hopper. Serving the Lord, I have only belonged to one other church besides the one I was in when I was saved. But one day, a friend asked if I would like to visit another church. I heard something in her voice that told me to go and visit that church. I'm one of those folks who will first check to make sure that what I want to do doesn't conflict with my church night.

The church is called Calvary Pentecostal Tabernacle. It wasn't a wealthy church. It was very small, but it was well established.

People there could easily hear from God. They moved in the word of the Lord. A lot of people went there for a word because it would come to pass a short time later. The waters of that church were sure.

It was the plan of God that I visited that church. The atmosphere there was unlike anything I had ever read about, been in, thought about, or heard. I knew something was very different. The Spirit of prophecy and the moves of God were in that church. There was such an atmosphere that I rushed up to the front.

There was such a presence of the Lord that the fear of the Lord came upon me. It took me into a place I had never entered before. The people there had angelic faces. I'm sharing this point because God wants to put Heaven upon our countenance. When He says, "Seek My face," He is telling us to seek out who He is.

A great reverence fell upon me in that church. Prophecy began to pour out. Direction came over the crowd. News was revealed. Prophecy brings light, development, and form. It puts life into dead things. It puts legs, health, clarity, and direction into the church.

There is a creative force that accomplishes what has been spoken and prophesied. Prophecy brings power. Something begins to happen in the heavens. We have to move the heavens to bring things into the earthly realm.

There was an unusual gift in our church. We declared the movements of the Lord. We often received reports about the words that we gave. One time, we heard a word about a big drug deal that was about to go down in the city. That was the prophecy. We got a rifle shot prayer.

Two or three days later, we read in the newspaper about some-one who was entrapped by the law. What do you do then? Well, you send the law of the Lord after them. The Bible says that the law of the Lord is perfect, converting the soul (Psalm 19:7). We want conversion in us. We want to be changed.

I stayed with that church for twenty-five years until I moved to Arizona. We continually studied for the vision, mind, and purpose of God. It was wonderful training. I never considered it to be difficult because I wanted to be a good missionary.

Our prayer life is a bit like having a marriage with the Lord. We are married to Him. When He says, "You haven't denied My name," He means, "You are married to Me. I can trust you at the gates. I can trust you in cities. I can talk to you and even My cor-rection will be like love words in your heart, because I know what is best for you."

This level of seeking and searching allows God to put the search light upon our heart. That is what He wants to do. Let God put people and nations upon your heart. Let Him burden you with what burdens Him. It becomes a natural thing. You will begin to see things and to prophesy.

SISTER RUTH PROPHESIES

It's Kevin again. Like Sister Ruth, you and I want to be around people whose gifts stir up your gifts. The gifts of the Holy Spirit are to be stirred up. Prophecy, seeing in the Spirit, is stirred up. The Word tells us that iron sharpens iron (Proverb 27:17).

Sister Ruth and I received prophetic words while we were filming episodes of the program *Stories from the Glory*. We would like to share some of them with you here. Open your heart to see what the Holy Spirit is saying to you through these messages. We pray that they will bless you and shed light on some of the important things we are facing in the days to come. Sister Ruth's testimony will begin this section.

(*Sister Ruth's testimony begins.*) I saw Brother Kevin in the Spirit. There was a shelf, like one you put books on. I saw this up above his head. It's a gold shelf. He was reaching up. God was giving him a lot of assignments. He has one prepared that will come with such an ease, because of the glory. Such ease!

It's going to fall into his hands. It's above him. This is what the Lord was saying. It's in the secret place. It's going to be the delight of your heart. It's going to be something that he hasn't shared.

God is going to turn things around. It's as if yesterday is going to come into today. Even what has already happened is going to come into today. The Lord is telling what He told me. He is saying to Brother Kevin that even if He could change your past, it doesn't make any difference for your future.

This word is good for everybody. God has great, mighty, and marvelous things for you. They are marvelous. Try to explain them. It will be difficult because of the glory that is upon what God is doing. It's going to appear suddenly. He has washed your eyes to see. He has salted your tongue to make people hungry and thirsty.

If we could only see how salt purifies. It keeps people from sliding, like when the ice is too thin. Hallelujah. God has given you an appetite for greater things. The glory of the Lord shall be revealed. The Lord says, "Just pull it down from Heaven."

Thank You, Father! Again and again, He has made things ready. Brother Kevin has passed a lot of tests in a short time. There are many grades he has accelerated above and beyond because of his obedience to the Lord. He has thrown off things that would have really made a difference to many. Remember that. Those things are no longer there. They're not in your mind or your vocabulary. They aren't saved for another day.

I see the love of God opening in Brother Kevin like a rose on a spring morning. It's the love of God, the wonderful essence of the Lord. He will be felt upon Brother Kevin. He will feel God's love come upon his life again and again.

This is what we want. We want to smell that fragrance and that fruitfulness of what God is doing. It's the fruit that we have in reserve. It shall remain in our life. He says, "I am coming for the precious fruit of the Earth" (James 5:7).

I saw Brother Kevin's heart. It was almost as big as the world. You will see that the healing touch will be applied to things. He is giving you that kind of heart. It won't break easily, except over God. It will break again and again over the Lord.

I see that He has a big steam press. Oh, He has His feet. There are many. God is going to press them in the wine. He is going to press the wrinkles in their garments. He is going to make them ready. Make ready. Prepare. Prepare a way for the Lord to come. This is very important. Prepare.

I recommend for everyone to just let go and let God. Let go of the old. Let go of the old way of ministry, the old way of thinking, and the old way of doing. Glean from the fields that are white unto harvest.

There is the enterprise of God. It's all right before you. You work it through your prayer life, through fasting, and through waiting upon the Lord. "Rise and shine, for the light has come and the glory of the Lord is risen upon you" (Isaiah 60:1). We are to allow this to happen. Make room for Him.

Because I am a woman, my voice hasn't always been strong. This is my natural voice. Today I don't need a microphone. Sing in the Spirit a lot. Sing! Let that expansion, that enlargement come inside to make room for the glory and to receive miracles. I see many unusual healings. That's what we are making room for. We are making room for more of Him.

Make room for more of the glory to come. It will gather the harvest. You don't have to look for open doors. In fact, you can't take care of them. You don't even carry a book. Be looking to see. We are to look. We are looking to see what Jesus is doing. We aren't looking in the natural.

He will give you witty inventions and new ideas you have never thought. He is doing it in the "now." It's right now. It will be at hand. It's the fulfillment that your heart has cried out for.

I saw in Brother Kevin where he has allowed his heart to break again and again for what God wants. He is about to pull back the curtain. I see there will be a great performance. The curtains are sapphire blue. I see it in the Spirit. He is pulling back the curtains. There will be betrayal. This isn't acting. This is action. There is a difference. It will suddenly come before you.

The ways of the Lord are going to appear on the right and on the left. That's because Brother Kevin is moving in the center fold of what God has ordained for his life. Thank You, Jesus. Thank You, Lord.

I also see this. When a man prepares to shoe a horse, he casts the shoe into the fire. Then he puts it on the racehorse. He is gathering the people who will run this race together.

Ladies, I am going to tell you that red is the shoe color to wear this season. It seems foolish, but the places we will be walking will be truly hot. I noticed that women at a conference were wearing red shoes. Brother Kevin's wife Kathi was wearing them. We will see into the prophetic realm. We are walking into that realm of the testimony of what God will do. We want that.

As we were filming, Brother Kevin shared some of the great things that God is about to do. The list went on and on, even after we were off the air. The glory of the Lord continued to reveal the greatness of what He is doing. Visions kept coming to such a measure that angels were in the room. They were whispering into our ears things that God wanted to do.

If we had stayed there all night, I believe that the river would have continued to flow. You see, that river is a song of the Lord. It *brings* from the throne. We don't want to say throne room. It brings from the *throne*. His throne is a moving chariot that covers the whole Earth.

God sees the whole Earth. He sees a total picture with everything in it, including all that is in our heart. Cry out to Him. John the Baptist said, "I'm just a voice." He cried out and the people came out to where he was.

Brother Kevin talked about the beings of Heaven, the nature around the throne, and the glory that is on the countenance of

Jesus. Oh, you could talk about that forever, because eternity is endless and we want to know who He is. Jesus should be our daily focus, our daily vision, and our whole heart.

Because I am with Him, I have seen the Lord. He carries it all. He gives me what I need on the right and on the left, wherever I go. He said, "I set before you the truth. I set before you all that I have. It's yours. But learn how to love Me. Just love Me. It will come through your returns, through your loving Me, and when you show your appreciation." God wants us to show appreciation for His greatness and for what He does for us.

Prophecy is only one of the gifts that reveal His glory. He has created us to know Him through many ways. He wants to come into our lives with a great enlargement and a great knowing that there is power.

Yes, there is power in the blood. That's where the power is. And there is power in His name. We are saved by His name, when we call upon His name (Romans 10:13). There is power in His Word that is above everything. There is power in everything He does.

We have only known the Lord in a small measure. But He said, "I'm going to show you. This is the fullness of time. It's what I'm doing and I want you to be part of it." We will begin to express the glory in many ways, including prophecy. It's the atmosphere of Jesus. The Spirit of prophecy is the testimony of Jesus (Revelation 19:10).

Every word coming out of your mouth will have eternal activity in it. You are speaking and declaring. You are putting things in order. Prophesy. Little prophesying is done in churches today.

Prophecy brings motion. It puts things in motion. It gets things going. We are to get busy and get moving. Praise God!

END TIME PROPHECY

Bless you all, saints. It's Kevin again. Sister Ruth and I have covered a lot of ground in this book. I know that we have answered some questions. You may have a few more questions that we haven't touched on yet. You can find the answers you need, if you will only seek the face of the Lord in His Word and in prayer.

What I want us to think about at this time are our end-time goals. As believers, do we even know where we stand with the Lord in this moment? Are we all ready to stand before Him if He returned today?

We are used to setting goals for ourselves in the natural world. We need to also have goals in our prayer life. We are meant to pray with purpose. We should always be praying from a standpoint of victory, of seeing the desired outcomes that we want. We should be praying from the heavenly realms. We are seated with Christ in the heavens.

We are to pray with purpose. That purpose is to glorify our heavenly Father. When we pray from a place of not knowing, a place of uncertainty, or from fear or a place of doubt or defeat, our prayers aren't effective. Think how much more powerful we are when we use our faith to say with full assurance:

"Thank You, Father, that You are moving. You are in control. You are taking care of *[insert concern]* right now!"

We know that God's eternal purposes were set in motion long ago. They are still playing out in the physical world—in particular concerning Israel.

At this time, we'd like to share some end-time prophetic words that we are receiving, to help you prepare for the moves of God that He has yet to reveal. As you read these words, listen for His voice. See what He is saying to you. I will begin with what I have received. After that, Sister Ruth will reveal what she has heard. We pray you will be blessed by these revelations.

(Editor's note: Remember that these prophecies were all pre-recorded. Kevin begins with his prophecy.)

Beginning with the Fall Feasts, there will be an access point for the body. There will also be a trigger that causes events to occur that will have a domino effect now and into the next year or more. The Lord has already spoken to me and to Sister Ruth about some of these things. There are some things that God wants us to do.

Revelatory gifts are going to manifest. Many people will receive these gifts. We have entered into the years of perfect vision. Discernment has come to the body of Christ. There will be eye-opening experiences that we will have in our spirit. *Ephesians 1:17-18* talks about the eyes of our heart being enlightened so that we may know.

The Spirit of seeing and knowing is coming upon the church. There is a Spirit of seeing, which is spiritual knowing, and there is a Spirit of hearing, where we hear what God is saying into the depths. I don't feel that people go deep enough. We need to be people of depth. We want to be quiet and listen.

People don't understand that we are entering into the times of the depths of God. The mysteries of the Spirit, which is Jesus Christ revealed, are part of that depth. The Word says, "Eye has not seen and ear has not heard what God has for those who love Him" (1 Corinthians 2:9). It says that it has been revealed to us by the Spirit of God.

I don't think people realized what we were entering into during the last part of 2020. The fire that is in our lives is causing us to be promoted. When that happens, our eyesight is healed. Jesus told me, "The reason why I am on the Earth right now is because people need to know that their eyes and their ears need healing."

People need to be able to see and hear in the Spirit. This is found in *1 Corinthians 2*. Paul wrote an entire chapter on the Spirit and about knowing. He said that a carnal person doesn't have any understanding about spiritual things. The end result of drawing near to the Lord is that people begin walking in seeing and knowing. People will become leaders.

There is a connection that has to be made. We must keep that connection in all that we do. God loves you and the connection must be made in love. If we don't take care of our physical body or feed it properly, it doesn't produce. Likewise, if we don't love and take care of the body of Christ, people won't produce. When we make and keep our connection with God, we will produce. We become part of the Word so that it can produce what it says it will.

The angel of the Lord has come to tell us that there is going to be a lot of healing, right now. He is telling me that this isn't the time to back off. It's not the time to have beach time. This is the time to have depth. It's a time to get out there into the deep. The healing that you are seeking is found in the depths. You need to soak in God's mercy and His love. He heals by His mercy. He heals because He has compassion for you.

God wants to reach out right now and touch you in compassion. He is having compassion upon people all over the world, right now. He is saying, "Come to Me. I am your Healer. Come to Me. Come to Me." He is the performer of the miracle. We need to come to Him and to rely upon His mercy and His love, right now.

There are all kinds of healings, right now. The Lord is handing out healings, right now. People need to turn around and get back into the boat. They need to get back out into the deep. They need to be with the Lord and to be wrapped up in Him.

It's amazing how much better it is going to get for you, if you would just go out into the deep. Jesus said, "Launch out into the deep for a catch" (Luke 5:4). The disciples put their nets down and pulled in a huge catch. The Lord is saying, "Launch out. Launch out into the deep." He says, "I will show you things that are happening around you. I will make you aware. I will be a hedge of protection. I will always be there."

Israel is the apple of God's eye. He wants us to be very involved with her. There is a remnant of people who know their God. The Lord says, "They will do exploits." We can hardly describe the greatness of what God is doing. But nations are being weighed down right now, concerning Israel. It's the work of the Lord.

Try to make a trip to Israel. Each time you go, He will announce something new. He will bring great change and a new order that always increases in size. The pressure seems to increase every time you go and come back. But He is changing you into His likeness, His purpose, and His move in the Earth.

God is weighing nations to see how they line up with Israel. He is seeing how they treat her. Do they support her? Give to her. If you can afford it, send someone there who wants to go. Be a part of others who are part of His vision concerning the whole world.

He said that He will not give up until He makes Jerusalem "a praise" in the Earth (Isaiah 62:7). We are to look to our beginnings and to the end of what God is doing. We are to be open to what He wants us to do and to go where He wants us to go.

God is doing this same weighing process in the body of Christ. Listen carefully. How God sometimes treats us may seem so minute, yet He is doing a big thing. We don't see what it is. It can be a hairpin thing, but when God triggers it, it opens to the bigger thing. So, we cannot neglect the little things that He tells us.

We can get visions sometimes, in a flash. That flash may be the key to what God wants to do. We have to be a people who are sensitive to God. He is gathering people of the same spirit and faith.

Many times it may feel like we are being confined. He may confine you. He knows what you want in the end, but you can't just do what you want. He needs us to be in a certain place. Our prayer life will be part of it. You may have to dismiss yourself from some people.

There is nothing wrong with entertaining one another or having dinner. I'm talking about going out *often*. We have to shut some of that down. We don't want to go out and start talking about other things, because it will diffuse the weight of the glory. It can cause a shortening or a stunting to the greatness of the glory.

We should be talking about the glory, like the two who were on the road to Emmaus. "Did you feel what happened today? What was your response? What did you hear?" We will ask one another for details about what the Lord is doing. We will feel the love and the goodness of God. We will want to talk about it. It will draw us into worship.

Get into worship like you have never known before. *Worship heals nations.* There will be great movements of people worshiping. It is going to sound like a flood coming upon the cities. It will wash the cities. God will bring people to the forefront who began in Him with a small birth.

There will be people who are given a new mantle. The glory will crown them. Angels will put crowns upon people. Read about Solomon being crowned and his time and position in the Earth.

Be a people who change the atmosphere wherever we go. This is extremely important. The atmosphere will change when God sends you because His presence is with you. We have to learn of His presence. We will feel the endorsement of the Lord. He will say, "Don't struggle with Me. I'm bringing you into My glory." You know, sometimes we try to get away from Him like a little child. But He is bringing His glory so that we will know His times and what He is doing in the Earth.

Whatever we need is coming into the Earth. Because we see Him, He has what we need and He will give it to us. But learn to live without some things. Learn to make adjustments so that your soul is seeking after the good of the land and the good of the nations. God is taking people of younger ages into the nations. I see missionaries being sent all over the world. I see new ministries being formed.

He is also giving people time to repent and time to do what He has ordained for them. He is increasing and enlarging people to see with the eyes of the Lord and to have an understanding of the days ahead. Their spirit is very quiet, but their vision is great.

People's names will be on a heavenly list, on a scroll. He says that your name is written on the palm of His hand. He knows you. He has called everyone. Be found in the part that has been chosen.

Many people are going to answer the call. God will give you the nations as a reward. If you are feeling the call and the fire in your belly and it starts pushing its way up into your throat when you read this prayer, then you are anointed to be a mouthpiece for God. He is calling you. Will you answer?

I see that the gold and the silver are going to start to appear again. There are going to be miracles, signs, and wonders in meetings. I saw that the gold is coming back. I am seeing ministries merging together and working together.

It is called a miracle. There are ministries that are merging together to bring in the harvest. The angels are going forth to different countries. They are breaking down the powers that are holding people back from knowing Jesus Christ.

This is a revolutionary time that we are living in. God is using the media and what we have in the media right now. I see people broadcasting all over the world. We are ready here at *Warrior Notes* to broadcast all over the world in every nation. We are going to go into every nation and we are going to broadcast the gospel and break the power of the devil! We are going to heal the sick and raise the dead!

There are women who want to have babies. Their wombs are opening up, right now. That's a miracle! The Lord told me that your womb is open, in Jesus' name. There are all kinds of people who have what looks like a band around their head. That's a demon that has been assigned to harass you in your generations. I break that curse, in Jesus' name. Your headaches are going. Your migraines are going.

The Word of the Lord is that the enemy is being driven out of your life. People are being delivered and healed. People with sores on their body are being healed. Some of you say that you have messed up and have made mistakes. The devil thought that he could stop you, but God has met you. You are set free, right now, in the name of Jesus!

There are going to be more weddings than normal. A lot of people will be married next year. God isn't going to wait any longer. He will put people together who are supposed to be together. There will be more weddings than normal because God is bringing people together.

He is saying, "Your land is married." You are getting married. It's not your fault. God has forgiven you and He is going to make it right. Next year will be a year of marriage and a year of agreement in marriage.

The Lord is saying, "I'm not waiting any longer. I'm going to move fast and you had better be ready." He is even telling me that we aren't going to be using the camels anymore. We are going to be using racehorses.

Great and mighty is your offspring in the Earth, like it says in *Psalm 112*. It says that great and mighty are the offspring on the Earth. That's your offspring. Your children are going to dance and spin and rejoice in the Lord. You may want to take a lesson from them.

Children love to dance and to worship. So, mothers, watch your children. They are going to be visited at night. They are going to start dancing and worshiping God. The angels showed me that part of the move of God would be with the children.

The children will start prophesying. I'm talking about five- and ten-year-olds. I saw children worshiping in the households. Their parents don't believe in that, but God is moving on the younger generation. This is going to begin happening right now.

Again, the Lord is saying, "Your land shall be married." He is going to restore everything back to you. Just wait and see what happens. There are all kinds of financial miracles that are happening, right now.

The Lord is turning over the rocks. There are hidden treasures that have been there all along. God is going to show you the hidden treasure. You will have financial miracles. He is going to favor you at your jobs. He will move people into the right job if they aren't in favor. He will move you. It will be so many people. You have no idea what is about to happen.

God is a good God. When He shows up, things have to listen to Him. Your circumstances will bow. You will watch them bow to the Lord Jesus Christ. Watch what happens. Demons are leaving people in droves. Oppression, depression, and all kinds of tormenting spirits are leaving people. You know, Christians can be oppressed and depressed. You can drive out devils. This is the Word of the Lord. The Lord has spoken a word over you. He's singing songs of deliverance over you right now, and those devils are leaving, right now. Thank You, Lord! Praise God.

I can see into the angelic realm. I saw what was going to happen. I saw angels coming down from Heaven and they are sweeping up and grabbing people by the arm. They are just whisking them to their destination. This is going to take place until the end. Three years ago, the angels of the Lord told me about this.

They said, "Kevin, don't ever wonder if you're in the perfect will of God. Because where we go, when we are sent to a person, you are in the center of God's will. That's because we showed up and because we were sent." They have been sent to implement this move of God. They said, "Don't wait. Jump in." For three years now, I have been doing that.

Unlike ever before, I feel the powers of the coming age, right now. The glory of the Lord is going to overshadow people. We are entering into the next year in the glory cloud. The move has already begun. We aren't to wait. We are to jump in now. The Lord says not to wait. The movement has already begun. I felt a shift that was so strong that I couldn't move. The angel of the

Lord has already gone before us and proclaimed our enemies as the enemies of God.

Whatever you are going through, the Lord has proclaimed that your enemies are His enemies. He has sent an angel to drive them out. Just receive this word right now. God is wrapping up all of the things that you need and that He will give you. God is going to shift your whole world.

There will be a tangible presence that begins at the end of the year and goes into the next year. God is going to initiate you into this final move. It is already happening. We are moving into the glory. The Lord is coming and He is going to want to be worshiped. We are going to honor Him and worship Him. Thank You, Father.

So many people are being healed. Arthritis is being healed, right now. I see all kinds of throat problems in those who were smokers—even those who quit years ago. The Lord is going to heal you of all of those symptoms that came from smoking. He has forgiven you and He is going to heal your throat. He is healing you right now.

Sinus problems are being healed. Blood sugar problems are being healed, right now. There is somebody whose left ear has been clogged. It is being opened right now, in the name of Jesus. Angel of the Lord, just go and open up ears, all over the world. Ears open, in Jesus' name. Eyes, if you are blind, the Lord is laying His hands on you. Receive your healing, right now. Eyes open, in Jesus' name. Thank You, Father.

Oh Lord, thank You for healing the people. Thank You for the compassion. You are reaching out and touching people all over the world. All kinds of skin and immune problems are being healed, right now. The angel of the Lord is going forth and the Lord is healing these problems.

I can hear people singing. There are so many people who are being delivered of demons, right now. All kinds of people are being delivered who have bad dreams at night and who are being harassed by evil spirits. The power of the Holy Spirit is breaking those enemies in your life, right now.

I saw the walls of China coming down. I saw China coming in. I saw multitudes from China coming in. It's going to happen. China is coming to the Lord. I saw a great revival there that cannot be contained. I am telling you that this next year is going to be a year of acceleration that people will talk about for a long time, so prepare yourself.

I have prophesied before that people need to get their oil lamps trimmed right now and that the light will shine. Keep the light bright. This is the time to get your oil. Get revelation of what God is doing.

This is the time to set yourself apart as a virgin and as a bride of the Lord. Get ready. Get everything ready. A time is coming that you are going to need that oil. You will need to have your wick trimmed. The bridegroom is coming. The bride must be ready!

Hear my voice. I am speaking from the very heart of God. You need to get ready *right now*. You need to get in the frame of mind that Jesus is coming back. He is going to whisk us into next year to do the harvest. The harvest is coming in. It is going to be an historic year, so stay with the glory cloud. Stay with the pillar of fire. Wherever God goes, just stay in the fire. Now let's look at what Sister Ruth sees prophetically, to help us prepare for our future.

(*Sister Ruth's prophecy now follows.*) There is an acceleration that is coming in the Spirit. God is doing a great, quick work. I am seeing new garments, mantles, and newness. There is nothing like newness. It is going to be so different. You are going to plug into it in the way you use your cell phone. You are going to hear from God. You will hear Him in your heart. You will see, hear, and then move on His words.

Let Him work. He will come. He will bring the wealth in. God knows how to do it. I am seeing people getting good reports from their doctors. They were going in and I could see God healing blood diseases. He's still working. I saw blood diseases. I saw platelets being put back into the blood.

Listen, take it. You receive it. Hear and receive it. Receive this healing. Thank You, Father. There are going to be seers. I believe God will have one in almost every family or in every church, in multiplication—a lot of children. There will be knowledge coming to the youth. They are going to have more visitations. Little children are going to speak like men of old. They will just start prophesying.

I'm talking about five-year-olds and ten-year-olds. I saw kids just worshiping in the households and the parents didn't even believe like that. God was moving on younger generations. This is all going to begin now. You will see it. It will manifest. It is coming alive. I see people coming alive. Don't wait. Jump in.

I had a vision twice of caskets around the altar. I thought, *What has happened? How many people have passed away? Has there been an accident?* I saw a little movement in one casket and a little movement over in another casket. Then I thought, *Oh, the people are alive. They just need to get out of this dead place. They need to get out of this place where they aren't moving.*

People feel the sickness, the weariness, and the tiredness. They are feeling the effectiveness of other people around them. Lay it all aside. Don't listen to it. Fine-tune your ears to hear what God has to say to you. Do something to move the hand of God.

Start laying hands on people. Lay hands on anyone who says they are ill or tired or weary. Say, "Let's touch God, brother. Let's touch God, sister. Let's see what God wants to do." Speak some faith into what you are hearing and saying. Trust God. He wants to manifest healing in your life.

I am seeing God. He is picking people. You know, there is a vision where the Lord picked up Ezekiel by the hair of his head. He picked him up by the locks of his hair. There was a covenant there. They had those long locks because of a covenant.

God will covenant with us. He wants to show us what is written. It is written. He wants you to wear it like a mantle upon your life. There are going to be gifts from God. He is going to come and unwrap and open up the gifts. Look into what God has for you.

I am seeing someone who has had a problem with their left foot, for a long time. It's like you have cracked a bone on the inside of the right arch of your left foot. It's on the right side of the foot.

God is going to mend it. He is going to heal it completely. You will never have pain in that foot again. Hallelujah.

I see someone who has made a new dedication. There has been urgency in your heart to follow the Lord and to be more dedicated to Him. I have seen where you are making an assertive effort. You are going to follow the Lord. You are going to obey the Lord. You are going to go in the direction that He is calling you into, which you can see.

I see blind eyes opening and cataracts being healed. I am seeing mothers who are widowed. I am seeing that this is going to be a wonderful time for you. This year will go out with an explosion and then come in with a shout of all of the new things that God is doing.

I see mothers and widows. Some are younger. You have lost your husband in the military, in war. There have been tragedies. You are going to have a new song in your heart. You are going to have a new skip and a new step of faith working in you.

You are going to feel the victory. You are going to feel the help of the Lord that you haven't felt or been aware of before. You are wondering where the substance or the help is going to come from. It will come from God. You are going to see the wonder of His ways and how He operates.

Your spirit will be so renewed. The days of mourning are over. He is going to pull it off of you and you are going to walk with your head up.

You are going to find that God is with you. He is always with you. I just see Him getting into the seed of things, deep into the seed. It's going to break open. God is nurturing those things you have planted in Him. You have been watering it. You will see a harvest that you haven't seen before. Hallelujah.

God is pulling on every vessel that will open itself unto Him to show us that He shall be magnified in the Earth. He shall be glorified. He is moving by His Spirit. It's not by might nor by power, but by His Spirit.

Cry out to God. Reveal yourself. Go after the Lord more than you would at a ball game. Come on. They are doing good there, but you can do better. Call out to God. Everyone, cry out to God! You have to have Him. Let your cry come from your heart.

Paul said, "That I might know Him" (Philippians 3:10). Oh, that I might know how to worship the Lord. It won't be lip service. It will be from the hearts that know their God.

I see God squeezing some of you, like you squeeze a tube of toothpaste. He is going to squeeze you until you release what He has given you. Don't you love that? Say, "Lord, squeeze me!" Just tell Him and let Him do it.

There is a beauty to the Lord that I see that is coming. I see these majestic colors. In those colors are revelation and knowledge. The revelatory wheel is found in the glory realm. Those are the eyes of the Lord. They call them wheels in the Bible, but they are the movements of God.

Wherever you go, people will begin to see. They will say, "I feel something. Something is happening in this room. What is happening?" These are the movements of God.

I would like to tell you a short story. There was a policeman who saw two cars go through each other. He said, "What happened?" He didn't see the cars until they came together at a light. He was sitting there grieving because he thought he had seen an accident.

He had screamed, "What's happening here? Something happened here! What happened here?" He said, "I *know* I saw an accident!" He saw the lady go through the red light, but God supernaturally took her through the other car.

That morning, I had phoned ahead at my prayer meeting before I arrived. I wasn't there yet, but I felt an urgency. I told the people, "You are to pray. I don't know what is happening, but I want you to pray, please, with all your might. I don't care if you scream at the top of your lungs. Pray with all your might!"

After I arrived, a man came to the meeting out of breath. I asked him, "What happened to you?" He said, "Sister Ruth, I was at a light. It was green. A lady on the other side ran a red light. I thought she was going to go right through me, but I looked and I couldn't find her! She was gone." The man could barely speak. His eyes were beholding the glory of the Lord that had rescued him. It was a movement of God.

God will do things not just so that you can see His glory. He will do them to spare you! He is going to keep you in His power. He will keep you to show you how much He cares for you. You will see how wonderful He is to you. This is the God that we are looking at.

Now I will return to the prophetic word. Do not be discouraged! Go with the flow. We are going through a time of transition. He said that He will do it. Look for it. Look for God in the ways that He works. Don't look at man. This is God's time. The knowledge of who He is will cover everything.

He is going to be faithful in all of our fears and in all of our tears. He will be glorious. In all of our lack, He will be great. You are going to see the greatness of God. Expect it! Get excited about it and tell Him that you are waiting. He will show Himself strong in you, with you, and for you.

He is giving strength to the older people, but He says that these are the good years. I see God destroying the horse and rider like He did in Egypt. I see Egypt being removed from people. Hallelujah!

You are not looking back and desiring the old or what you had before. He wants freshness in the Spirit. The bride is preparing. She has made herself ready. Let's make ourselves ready. He is doing this because He is opening up the gates.

I see the colors of the rainbow, the promises of God. You are going to fight this battle with great ease, and you are going to see through the victories. You will see enlargement in the Spirit. You will see gain, even in the natural, things you have needed.

You are going to see God coming with a blessing. This is going to be the blessing. The winning prizes are coming. In many ways, there is going to be a new structure in the Spirit. I see God blowing upon nations. He is brooding over nations.

He is getting ready to cause people to rise and shine and leap forward. Just step into your house. Cross the threshold in one of your rooms and say, "Yes, this is a prophetic act of stepping into it." Step with joy! Let the joy of the Lord come upon you for the strength that you need.

There is restoration everywhere. I see that angels are being put to work. You are going to know it. You are going to feel the vibrations of it. You are going to feel the nearness of the coming of the Lord. He is right here upon you, but He will allow you to enjoy the benefits of what He is doing.

You wait, not as those who have no hope. You work, not as those that have no reward. You are waiting for the coming of the Lord. Also, this is a strange vision. I've been in one of the pyramids of Egypt. It wasn't easy going in. You had to bow very low to go in there. In fact, I was a little concerned about coming back out.

I saw people coming out of Egypt. I saw where they have been trying to get out. They are coming out. I see activity everywhere. I see movement—a movement of God's Spirit. People will be reporting all of the victories that are coming. Hallelujah!

Brother Kevin will confirm that he saw people's faces just shining and glowing in the Lord as they walk into that newness. This is the time. This is the transition time. God has ordained this. This was spoken to Brother Kevin three years ago by angels.

An Imparation

Friends, it's Kevin again. At this time, I would like to share a prayer of impartation that Sister Ruth has prayed over the people who were listening in on our initial broadcast. Remember that impartation is given by the Holy Spirit, and He is not dependent upon our time frame. God, His Word, His Holy Spirit, and His anointing are eternal.

(Sister Ruth's prayer of impartation now follows.)

Many angels will be dispatched through this prayer. Lord, send many for many nations. You will have a representative and we thank You for it. They will know it. They will get ready. They will prepare. They will put aside the old so that the new can come forward. God, thank You for the vision.

Lord, You will pick them up. You will carry them. You said You picked up Ezekiel by the locks of his hair. You had a covenant with him. You have a covenant with these people that You want to send quickly, for the hour is very late. The day is short. Now, God, we just speak it into existence, that You will send them on Your chariots. Lord, You will amaze them at the victories and the help and the moments that will come.

Lord, in a moment, You will shoot them like an arrow. They will be Your arrow of truth in the land. They will be Your song of praise, Your burden of peace, that You are bringing into the nations. We declare it over each one that has heard the Word.

Lord, I have asked You, "Who can I pass this mantle to?" I am seeing it. I see priests coming forward and people at the altar. I see the bells. They are the biggest bells I have ever seen. They have been in the holy place. They have been in the secret place.

You have been seeking the face of God and saying, "When? When Lord, when?" This is "when." This is the time. The winds are blowing again. The winds are stirring nations.

Lord, we thank You for the ministry of helps. Lord, that those who stay at home will have the same reward. We thank You, God, that we are all working together for Your good and for Your purposes. And we give You praise and honor for all You shall do, in Jesus' name. Amen.

I am seeing Mexico right now. I saw all these chili peppers. It's Mexico. Mexico, get yourself ready. Prepare the way of the Lord. Prepare it. The Lord is coming in His glory. He is coming in His honor. He is coming with His concern, His care, and His safety, even as you turn to Him with all of your heart. Turn away from the fundamentals of religion. Know God.

Cause them to turn unto You with all of their heart, Lord, so that You can do the things You want to do in the nations. You want a new baptism, a Spirit of truth, like a carpet rolled out to them, in the name of Jesus. We thank You for it. Thank You, Lord.

Many of you will learn the language. I see people learning Spanish in a moment. You are fasting and praying and God is going to give you the language so that you will be able to speak to the people.

Thank You, Jesus. Thank you, Lord. Coliseums will be open. God will have great platforms and gatherings in the streets. I see little fires on the streets, in shops, and in stores. God has started a new fire. God, send Your Word one more time. Send Your Word even to those, God, who are blind and cannot see spiritually. Open their eyes. Anoint their eyes. God, give them a second chance. Give them, Lord, another day to crowd to You and to be moved, in Jesus' name. Amen.

CLOSING PRAYER

Hallelujah saints, this is Kevin. Glory! The Lord has spoken to us all here. I extend a warm "thank you" to Sister Ruth Carneal for sharing the intimate aspects of her spiritual walk, as well as her extensive travels. We have already filled an entire book with her wisdom and insights, and yet we have barely touched on her experiences.

Friends, be confident in knowing that God knows exactly where you are, right now. It doesn't matter what part of the world you are in. God knows your address. He has a divine book that is already written about you!

In *Psalm 139:16,* it says that each one of your days was written in a book before one of them even came to pass. Jesus loves you. God has sent His Word and healed you. He has sent the Holy Spirit to comfort you. Your Father in Heaven loves you. Always trust in Him. Always put your faith in Jesus Christ.

No matter what you are going through in life, God isn't going to leave you as an orphan. Jesus promised that the Holy Spirit would come and never leave you. So just receive God's love right now.

The blood of Jesus forgives you of all of your sins. Your past is wiped away! If you haven't accepted Jesus as your Savior, you can make Heaven your home right now. Just receive Jesus Christ as your Savior. Acknowledge Him as the One who took your place on the cross. Acknowledge Him and call upon His name right now, wherever you are. I see many people getting on their knees. Just raise your hands and say this simple prayer of faith:

"Jesus, You are the way. You are the truth, and You are the life. I give my life to You, right now."

Just say it. If you believe that you are reading this right now because God has set this up for you, then you need to give your life over to Jesus Christ. He has a wonderful plan for you!

Psalms 139:5 and 85:13 reveal that the Lord has prepared a pathway for you and He stands in your future. He has also gone behind you and will protect you from the hurts of your past. The Lord's thoughts toward you are many and great. He has set His boundaries in your life for a reason. They are there because He loves you and He wants to keep you. Receive Him and step into the glory realm. He is waiting for you there, with open arms. God bless you all.

Glory Notes

T HESE ARE BRIEF summaries of the topics discussed in each chapter. Feel free to study each one at your leisure to determine your strengths and weaknesses walking in the glory. We have found that keeping a journal as we listen for the voice of the Lord is very helpful. The more time you spend in prayer and listening for God's voice, the more revelation you will receive. God bless you in your walk!

CHAPTER ONE

- Be Hungry for the Lord
- Hasten to Do
- Follow Instructions Carefully
- Study the Word
- Fast
- Pray

CHAPTER FOUR

CHAPTER FIVE

Salvation Prayer

Lord God,
I confess that I am a sinner.
I confess that I need Your Son, Jesus.
Please forgive me in His name.
Lord Jesus, I believe You died for me and that You
are alive and listening to me now.
I now turn from my sins and welcome You into my
heart. Come and take control of my life.
Make me the kind of person You want me to be.
Now, fill me with Your Holy Spirit who will show
me how to live for You. I acknowledge You before
men as my Savior and my Lord.
In Jesus' name. Amen.

If you prayed this prayer, please contact us at
info@kevinzadai.org for more information and material.
Go to KevinZadai.com for other exciting ministry materials.

Join our network at Warriornotes.tv. Join our ministry and
training school at Warrior Notes School of Ministry.

Visit KevinZadai.com for more info.

ABOUT KEVIN L. ZADAI

Kevin Zadai, Th.D. was called to ministry at the age of ten. He attended Central Bible College in Springfield, Missouri, where he received a bachelor of arts in theology. Later, he received training in missions at Rhema Bible College and a doctorate of theology from Primus University. He is currently ordained through Rev. Dr. Jesse and Rev. Dr. Cathy Duplantis.

At age thirty-one, during a routine day surgery, he found himself on the "other side of the veil" with Jesus. For forty-five minutes, the Master revealed spiritual truths before returning him to his body and assigning him to a supernatural ministry.

Kevin holds a commercial pilot license and is retired from Southwest Airlines after twenty-nine years as a flight attendant. Kevin is the founder and president of Warrior Notes School of Ministry. He and his lovely wife, Kathi, reside in New Orleans, Louisiana.